GUIDE
TO
TAROT

GUIDE
TO
TAROT

Sarah Kettlewell

CAXTON REFERENCE

© 2000 Caxton Editions

This edition published 2000 by Caxton Editions,
20 Bloomsbury Street, London, WC1B 3QA.

Caxton Editions is an imprint of the Caxton Publishing Group.

Printed and bound in India.

CONTENTS

INTRODUCTION

How often have we wondered what the future holds in store for us, or reached a crossroads in our lives when we would give anything just to gain an inkling into the consequences of a decision or event, or wondered if happiness, romance, wealth or travel are heading our way?

By nature, we human beings are extremely inquisitive where our futures are concerned. More and more of us visit fortune tellers and avidly read our horoscopes in the hope of providing insight in to a variety of life questions.

Tarot reading has become increasingly popular as a means of predicting the future, due in no small part to the cards themselves. We respond intuitively to the beautifully illustrated images and are intrigued by the mystery and romance surrounding the cards.

There is more to Tarot reading than simply asking a question, dealing the cards and then looking up a book for the answer. We all possess some capacity for 'gut-feeling' or 'hunches' which, without anything tangible to support them, we often ignore. Tarot is a means of grasping this intuitive capacity and developing it as a means of guidance.

This book aims to offer advice for the beginner in understanding and interpreting the cards, however the real knowledge comes from practice, from memorising the layouts, and the meanings behind each card to the moment when we can form our own style of interpretation when we can make sense of a seemingly random selection of cards in response to elements surrounding a person's life.

HISTORY OF TAROT

There is mystery and controversy surrounding the exact origins of the Tarot. For some, Ancient Egyptian mysticism holds the key, whilst others have seen connections with China and India, and certainly there is evidence supporting all theories in the quest to discover how the cards we know today came into being.

Historically, Tarot is first seen in medieval Europe, when it was brought over from India by the gypsies, although it is widely held that its origins date much further back.

Gypsies began migrating from India in the 9th century, arriving in Europe around 500 years later. They brought with them their Hindu culture and custom, one of which was the use of cards, depicting religious images. These sacred cards were beautifully illustrated and the symbols were used to teach key elements of the Hindu faith, and to educate an almost entirely illiterate audience.

As the gypsies' migration continued, so did the Tarot's. The deck was now being used to predict the future and also for playing card games. Indeed, one of the earliest records of the existence of the name 'Tarot' is in medieval Italy when a card game with the French title of *'les tarots'* was played. However, it is not this likely-sounding game which bears most resemblance to the deck we know today, but another popular card game, also played in Italy around this time, called *tarocchi* which was played following similar rules to bridge. The earliest, and almost completely preserved, deck of tarot cards is the famous Visconti-Sforza deck, which was produced in the mid 15th century.

This deck is the first indication of the familiar 78 card deck and comprised of 22 cards of the Major Arcana and the 56 cards of the Minor Arcana. The members of the Visconti-Sforza family posed as models for the pictures of the Major Arcana. Their coats of arms are visible and legend has it that they symbolise persons and events belonging to 15th- century Milan.

The symbolism used in Tarot takes its imagery from many different beliefs and cultures. As we have discovered, the origins of Tarot are not easily traced. however we do know that the Tarot we know today was born at a time when many trains of thought were converging in Europe and it is safe to say Tarot is not the result of only one or two influences.

The designs were executed in Europe, and contain imagery directly linked not only to the Christian and Islamic religions, but also Celtic and Norse to culture. The Tower, for instance, suggests parallels with the Norse Hammer of Thor, or the lightning flash of enlightenment, described in Mahayana and Tantric Buddhism, when all illusions are destroyed. The Star, Moon and Sun are descended from Arabian and Classical astrology, the Lovers includes the pagan figure of Eros, and the Judgement card depicts an apocalyptic scene common to both the Christian and Muslim faiths. By the late 18th century, Tarot had become extremely popular in revolutionary France, probably as a result of the desire to grasp some sense of hope in extremely volatile and unstable times, and became the focus of an occultist by the name of Antoine de Court Gebelin (1723-87). In his publication *Monde Primitif* in 1781, he asserted that the Major Arcana was directly linked to the Ancient Egyptian Book of Thoth – 'Thoth' being the Egyptian god of science, wisdom and mysticism. Legend has it that this book was rescued from the great fire of Alexandria and was the synthesis of all human knowledge with deep mysticism.

Connections to the ancient mystical Jewish tradition of Kabbalah were made by another Frenchman by the name of Eliphas Levi (1810-75) who in the 19th century was famous for his books on magic. This interest in the darker, more mysterious side to Tarot made the cards extremely popular with magical orders, and occult groups, the most famous and influential being the Hermetic Order of the Golden Dawn, a secret occult society based in London between 1888-1900. This group included many leading literary figures such as Bram Stoker and W. B. Yeats and 2 of the Order's members, Arthur Waite and Pamela Colman Smith, later produced the revolutionary Rider-Waite deck, published in London in 1910 by Rider & Co. (hence the name Rider-Waite). This is today the most commonly used deck and is the one we will be referring to throughout the course of this book. The deck was revolutionary in that up until this time the Minor Arcana's cards had no illustrations on them other than a symbol and a number, i.e the 5 of cups had 5 cups and nothing more. Waite devised recognisable images for each of the 56 cards and as a result, all 78 cards in the Rider-Waite deck have a general symbolism, although the Major Arcana is more profound.

Another famous exponent of Tarot was the occultist Aleister Crowley (1875-1947) who developed a deck known as the Thoth Tarot.

The late 20th century has seen a dramatic increase in the popularity of the Tarot, with new decks being created all the time. Indeed, the Surrealist artist Salvador Dali produced a Tarot deck as one of his works of art. Decks today could be described as works of art themselves, varied as they are in their symbolism, beautifully illustrated, drawing their inspiration from many different sources.

WORKING WITH TAROT CARDS

Rituals surrounding the use of Tarot cards are to be expected, and it is up to the individual user how far he or she adheres to them. Legend has it that the cards will not work unless they are kept wrapped in a piece of silk, which is believed to prevent the cards being contaminated with adverse forces from their surroundings, and that you must never let anyone else use your cards. This adds to the mystery of the cards that so intrigues us, and certainly treating them with respect and observing a little ritual can aid the user in moving to a quieter, more concentrated state of mind removed from the hustle and bustle of everyday life. The psychological state of the user is vital to to the success of a reading. If we are emotionally unsettled in any way, this will affect our interpretation of a spread.

Choosing a Deck

As we have seen earlier, our intuitiveness is a key element in Tarot reading. Therefore, we cannot underestimate the importance of choosing a deck that feels 'right' to us. There are an enormous amount of decks to choose from and, to the novice, one may seem as good as another. Take time to find a deck which you feel you can respond to, whose images stimulate your imagination, in short one you can basically develop a relationship with!

It is advisable to the novice to choose the most commonly used decks such as the Tarot de Marseilles, the aforementioned Rider-Waite, or the Morgan-Greer. This is basically because most publications for the beginner to consult will refer to these decks. If you are having trouble obtaining a pack which suits there are some useful addresses on page237 of suppliers that stock a large range of cards.

As mentioned, it is up to the individual user whether or not to accept esoteric explanations for the rituals surrounding the storage and use of the deck. Certainly, to keep the cards safe, the practice of wrapping them in silk and storing in a wooden box is advisable. Whether you believe by doing this you will protect the cards from undesirable vibrations, wear and tear or prying little hands is up to you.

Preparing for a Reading

When preparing for a reading, it is important to create an atmosphere which will allow both the querant and the reader to remain focused. By following these simple steps, you will manipulate your tarot reading environment to best effect:

●   Wherever possible, have only yourself and the

querant present, this will allow a much more honest interpretation of the cards without any disruptive and conflicting vibrations from any 'spectators'.

- Spend some time beforehand creating an atmosphere which focuses on the area where the cards are to be read. (Some readers keep a small wooden table which they use only for readings.) Close the curtains to block out any outside distractions, and light some candles close to the table.

- Have the reading area as quiet as possible, no television or radio.

- Have the querant sit facing south, while you face north. This is because, in Esoteric law, the hidden currents of the earth flow from north to south and back again, therefore the centre of power and authority is in the north. (Interestingly, in Ancient China, the magistrates always sat at the north end of the court, the felons at the south.)

- If your cards are wrapped in silk, make sure it is large enough to cover the area of a spread, so the cards can avoid contact with the table top.

These preparations may seem a little elaborate or superstitious, but they do help to concentrate the mind before a reading.

There are a variety of layouts or spreads which can be used to gain insight into our lives through the tarot deck. In the following chapter, we will study a selection of spreads which I believe are the most useful for the beginner.

Handling and Shuffling the Cards

The reader should shuffle the cards thoroughly, turning some of them from top to bottom at regular intervals to ensure a mixture of upright and reversed cards. The cards are then handed to the querant in order for he or she to shuffle them again remembering to reverse some of the cards. Pay particular attention to the orientation of the deck when the querant is shuffling the cards as it is vital the cards face the same direction for you as for them. So, if the querant is seated facing south, the cards will be in reverse, therefore you, the reader, must turn them so they are facing the same way as for the querant.

- The querant cuts the deck twice using their left hand which is considered to be closer to the heart and therefore embodiesthe true character of a person.

- The first cut is then placed to the left of the remainder of the deck, then the process is repeated to give three piles of cards.

- Reassemble the deck in the same order, that is, from right to left so that the original stack is placed on the first cut, which is in turn placed over the second cut.

- The number of cards required for a reading can now be taken from the top of the pack.

Fanning the Cards

If the querant is required to select a number of cards:

- The whole deck must be spread out in a line face-down across the table.

- The required number of cards are chosen by the querant.

- The reader should pay attention to the sequence in which the cards are chosen as they must be subsequently laid out in the same order for a reading.

Laying out a Spread

When laying out the cards for a reading, they are placed face down. When turning over the cards, it is imperative they are turned from side to side, as opposed to from top to bottom. This way, they will not be inadvertently reversed, and their subsequent interpretation will be a true reflection of the spread. Once all the cards have been turned, the reading can begin.

Significators

Significators are common in tarot readings and are the court cards of the Minor Arcana. They are drawn before a reading to represent the querant. When selecting a Significator, the following points should be considered:

- The querant's astrological sign
- The querant's sex and age
- The querant's physical appearance

The Significators are as follows:

Wands			
CARD	ASTRO SIGN	AGE	APPEARANCE
King	Aries, Leo Sagittarius	Over 35 Male	Red/Fair hair Hazel/Grey eyes
Queen	As above	Over 35 Female	Red/Fair hair Brown/Blue eyes
Knight	As above	Under 35 Male	Fair hair Grey/Blue eyes
Page	As above	Youth Male/female	Red/Fair hair Blue eyes

Swords			
CARD	ASTRO SIGN	AGE	APPEARANCE
King	Gemini, Libra, Aquarius	Over 35 Male	Black/Dark hair Dark eyes
Queen	As above	Over 35 Female	Fair hair Grey eyes
Knight	As above	Under 35 Male	Dark hair Dark Eyes
Page	As above	Youth Male/female	Fair hair Blue eyes

Cups			
CARD	ASTRO SIGN	AGE	APPEARANCE
King	Pisces, Cancer, Scorpio	Over 35 Female	Fair hair Blue eyes
Queen	As above	Under 35 Male	Brown hair Blue eyes
Knight	As above	Under 35 Male	Brown hair Grey/Blue eyes
Page	As above	Youth Male/female	Brown hair Brown/Blue eyes

Pentacles			
CARD	ASTRO SIGN	AGE	APPEARANCE
King	Taurus, Virgo, Capricorn	Over 35 Male	Black/Dark hair Dark eyes
Queen	As above	Over 35 Female	Black/Dark hair Dark eyes
Knight	As above	Under 35 Male	Brown hair Dark eyes
Page	As above	Youth Male/female	Brown hair Dark eyes

The Significator cards are fairly general in their interpretation, and it can prove problematic to choose one which fits in precisely with all the attributes of the querant. Therefore, if a Significator is to be used, compromise is necessary. For instance Page of Wands may be selected to represent a young girl born under a fire sign, even though she may not possess all the physical elements of this particular card.

Once the Significator has been chosen, the card may be left out to act as a focus for the reading, or left in the deck, in this case, when the deck is split, only the half containing the Significator is used.

Interpreting a Layout

It is now time to put all your knowledge to the test. It can be an intimidating experience for the beginner when faced with their first 'real' reading with a querant, particularly a stranger. There is no substitute for practice, and it is recommended that you have spent considerable time examining the cards and their interpretations, in different spreads. As shown in the following chapter, there are many different spreads from which the reader can choose, depending on the information the querant requires. With practice, an overall 'feel' for the spreads will become easier, as associations between the cards and their reversed or upright meanings become more apparent.

An experienced reader can connect intuitively experiences which appear completely unrelated, and to do this it is essential the novice starts with relatively basic spreads. There are straightforward yet comprehensive layouts which involve four cards or fewer which are ideal starters. These will greatly enhance interpretative skills and make for a much more convincing, stress-free reading.

When reading the cards, there is an understandable tendency to isolate the cards and interpret them individually to the point where the reading becomes rather mechanical and impersonal. Merely relating the individual meanings of the cards makes for a less than satisfactory reading. To overcome this, it is vital to interpret the spread as a whole.

There are various techniques which can be employed to do this:

- A predominance of Minor Arcana cards will dictate the theme of the reading. The Suits' themes are as follows:

Many Wands	= Career/Work Issues
Many Cups	= Emotions and Affairs of the Heart
Many Swords	= Intellectual Affairs
Many Pentacles	= Material Affairs

  The Suits have opposites as follows:
  Wands(fire) are opposite to Cups (water).
  Swords (air) are opposite to Pentacles (earth).

Their interpretation will therefore be modified depending on their neighbouring cards. For example, the meaning will be enhanced if the neighbouring cards are of the same suit and weakened if they are of the opposite suit.

- The presence of many cards from the Major Arcana indicates important events for the querant which will be of great significance in his or her life. These can often be influences and experiences which are outside the querant's control.

- If Major Arcana cards are surrounded by

those of the Minor Arcana, their meaning
will very much depend on the meaning of the
lesser cards and whether they are upright or
reversed.

- A large number of reversed cards indicate the
  way forward will be full of difficulties and
  obstacles which will have to be overcome.

- The presence of many court cards from the
  Minor Arcana indicates the effect others
  have on the querant's life, and their actions
  and influences will play a huge role.

- When interpreting a card, be sure to take into
  consideration its position in the spread and
  the cards surrounding it.

Helpful Hints for the Novice

Tarot reading carries with it a certain responsibility
toward the querant. It is vital to be professional at all
times and to conduct a reading confidently. As
mentioned, spending time with the cards, rehearsing the
layouts and the meanings of the cards are imperative for
a successful reading. The querant needs to be
comfortable with the reader and safe in the knowledge
that they know what they are talking about!

The very nature of the cards and their origins are
mystery enough. There can be a temptation to be over-

dramatic when conducting a reading which can be detrimental to the process. Avoid this as it can make the querant feel ill at ease, or encourage scepticism; either way it will not make for a productive reading.

Try to be sensitive toward the querant and gauge their reaction to what you are saying. If they become unsettled at any point, do not be afraid to temper your interpretations. This is particularly important in the case of a predominantly negative layout. Even if the overall theme of the reading is really dreadful, never predict catastrophes such as death or serious illness.

BASIC SPREADS

As stated, there are a number of Tarot spreads which can be used for simple 'yes', 'no' questions, as well as much more elaborate layouts which can offer a more detailed insight into a situation or difficulty experienced by the querant. These vary from very simple two or three card spreads to more complicated layouts which can utilise over twenty cards.

One Card

Of the more basic readings the 'yes', 'no' questions are ideal for the novice tarot reader. This direct and simple way of reading the tarot concentrates upon the querant's question or situation. The first of these is the One Card short question. The querant should draw one card from the Major Arcana. The chosen card will signify the situation surrounding the theme of the question. The symbolism of the card allows the reader to give insight into the querant's situation. In order to see what kind of week or day a querant may have, a card can be chosen without asking a question. This method will allow the reader to learn how to convert the cards into meanings for everyday life.

The Two-Card Spread

As confidence grows, the reader may wish to develop into using the Two-Card Spread.

This is basically an extension of the One or Short Card Question, and utilises cards from the Major Arcana only. First, the querant is asked to concentrate on an issue or question and to draw a card from the Major Arcana. Then, to gain an insight into how the situation will develop, a second card is drawn.

The Three-Card Spread

By using a Three-Card Spread, the issue or question at the centre of the reading will be viewed from the past, present and future.

Card 1 draws influences from the past, Card 2 concentrates on the present and Card 3 for future developments. This is a particularly useful reading for the novice reader, as, again, it concentrates on cards solely from the Major Arcana. These three short spreads give valuable experience and insight in translating the cards from the Major Arcana, and with practice, the reader will grow in confidence.

  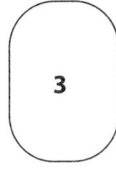

Past	Present	Future
The current position	A possibility or problem	The outcome of the interaction of these

The Four-Card Spread (or the Cross)

This is the final layout of cards using only the cards from the Major Arcana. The four cards are drawn and laid out in the form of a cross.

The order of the cards is:

Card 1: The theme of the reading, and what surrounds it.

Card 2: Options to be considered by the querant regarding this matter.

Card 3: Options not to be considered.

Card 4: The consequences.

The advantage of the Four-Card spread, is that it contains a cautionary note for the querant in Card 3. This spread can be done using the Major Arcana only, but can also be done using the whole deck. When the whole deck is used, it is important to note that should a card from the Major Arcana appear, this will be the main indication, the strongest influence.

If using the whole deck for The Cross, the situation of a Major Arcana card will be significant, as follows:

Card 1: If the Major Arcana card falls here, then the theme of the question will be of vital importance to you.

Card 2: Your course of action must be considered very carefully indeed, the consequences are too important to ignore.

Card 3: There will be a temptation to make the wrong decision, beware!

Card 4: The consequences of your actions will be very important to you.

The more cards of the Major Arcana, the more

significant the theme will be. These cards emphasise the fact that this question or dilemma is more important than you perhaps thought. The cards of the Minor Arcana carry less significance.

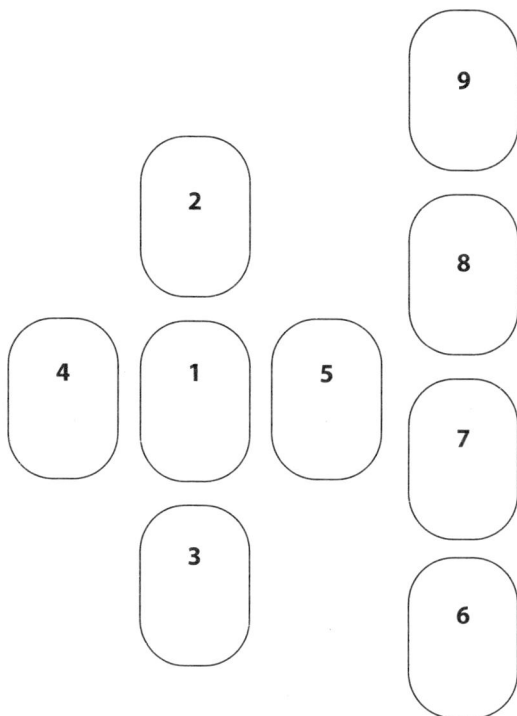

The Nine-Card Spread

The cards will have been shuffled by you, then by the querant as described above. The cards are then laid face-down in the order and pattern as shown in the illustration opposite. The cards should be turned and interpreted one at a time. The cards' significance is as follows:

Card 1:   This card signifies the most prominent feature of the querant's current situation.

Card 2:   This card indicates the best possible outcome which can be attained at this time.

Card 3:   This card represents underlying or hidden elements which are affecting the situation in question. This could be the background to the whole situation.

Card 4:   This card is representative of the past, and the effect past actions have had on the present situation.

Card 5:   This indicates the probable outcomes if no action is taken and no change of direction takes place.

Cards 6–9: These four cards give an insight to what the near future holds. The cards can be taken in sequence, that is the 6th card being the immediate future, the 9th the more long-term.

Ideally, this reading should be done without any prior consultation with the querant. In this way a truer, completely unbiased translation is possible.

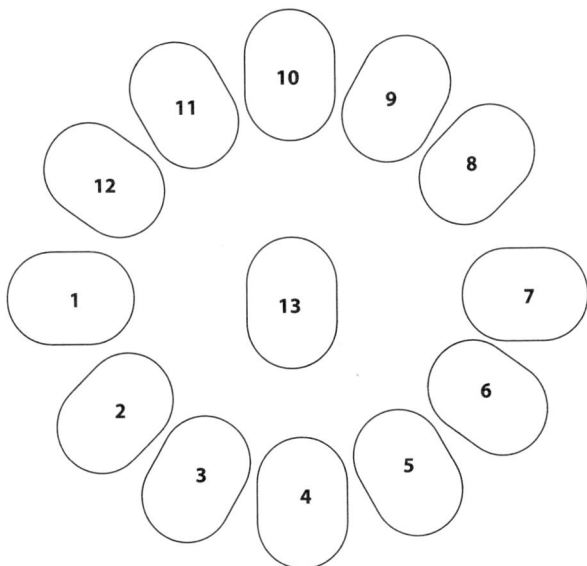

The Circular Spread

The Circular Spread is considered to be one of the most reliable for giving a forecast for the year ahead, beginning from the date of the reading itself. After the cards have been shuffled, as described above, follow this procedure:

●   Working from the top of the pack, deal out twelve cards face upward in a circle, then lay the 13th card in the centre, also face upward, (see illustration on above). This last card is important as it gives the overall theme of the forecast. This card should be interpreted first.

● Next, interpret the other twelve cards in sequence, moving around the circle anti-clockwise.

Below is an example of a reading following the Circular Spread. (If the top of the card is facing in towards the centre of the circle, this means the card is Upright or Dignified.) The card in the centre is the Ten of Wands. This card signifies overcommitment and oppression suggesting the excessive burdens of taking on too much work. The querant may be facing new responsibilities as a result of an expansion or promotion, and is struggling to keep up with the demands placed on him or her from work and home. This is the theme for the forecast.

Card 1: The first card in the reading is the King of Pentacles. This refers to the month ahead and indicates a mature man who will be influential. The King of Pentacles is a practical, reliable character who is often an employer. His presence signifies the possibility of an improvement in the querant's finances and a possible promotion at work.

Card 2: The second card refers to conditions two months hence. In this case the card is the Five of Swords. This card indicates a conflict which the querant is likely to lose. The result of this is a period of low self-esteem and there will be a temptation to feel negative and give up. However, if defeat is accepted gracefully, the querant will emerge stronger and be able to move on to pastures new, stronger from the experience.

Card 3: The third card is The Magician. This Major Arcana card has added weight and signifies an important stage in the querant's life three months hence. The Magician indicates renewed confidence and excellent communication skills which will push good ideas into positive action. This card signifies a successful period for the querant.

Card 4: The King of Swords indicates a strong, authoritative male influence who will prove to be of great assistance four months hence.

Card 5: The Two of Wands. This is an extremely optimistic card to draw and signifies the successful attainment of goals. It is indicative of deserved financial rewards, and highlights positive partnerships.

Card 6: The Empress. The Major Arcana card adds weight to the significance of this month. Her presence in the reading indicates that six months hence the querant will enjoy a period of satisfaction and harmony, particularly relating to physical and emotional issues, family and the home.

Card 7: The Knight of Cups. This card points to new initiatives involving the querant, quite possibly regarding his or her personal relationships, or creative pursuit.

Card 8: The Four of Pentacles (reversed). This card points to greed and fear of loss, mainly material.

Card 9: The ninth card is the Five of Wands. This card traditionally signifies strife and aggravation. This will relate to the message of the previous card. The querant must overcome feelings of anxiety and frustration to succeed.

Card 10: The Nine of Pentacles (reversed). This card warns against compromising material security. In relation to the previous card, it advises against turning to dubious practices in an effort to succeed.

Card 11: The Six of Swords. This card indicates better times have arrived. The querant is now able to put the problems of the past behind. However, this card reminds the querant there will still be trouble ahead, even though the worst is over. A long journey, perhaps over water, is also indicated.

Card 12: Temperance. This final Major Arcana card is the last one in the reading. It shows the harmonious conclusion of the year's events, when the querant will handle any problems well through careful consideration and self-control.

The Horseshoe Spread

When the answer to a particular problem or question is desired, the Horseshoe Spread can be recommended to offer a straightforward yet comprehensive insight.

Shuffle the cards as described above, then let the querant shuffle, whilst concentrating on the specific question he or she wants to ask.

Take the cards from the querant, and, with the cards facing downwards, deal seven off the top of the pack face upwards.

The cards are now ready to be read in a clock wise direction, left to right.

Card 1: Refers to the past.

Card 2: Refers to the present.

Card 3: Refers to the future.

Card 4: Indicates the best direction for the querant to follow.

Card 5: Reveals the attitudes of those close to the querant.

Card 6: Points to obstacles standing in the way.

Card 7: Indicates the probable and final conclusion.

Below is an example reading from a 33 year-old woman

at a cross-roads in her career who has been offered a new position with another company. The question is "What will be the outcome of a job move?"

The cards fall as follows:

Card 1: **The King of Pentacles:** This represents a strong male influence who was instrumental in the querant's success and happiness at work in the past.

Card 2: **The Five of Wands:** Represents the anxiety currently experienced by the querant and the limits which have been imposed on her.

Card 3: **The Four of Pentacles** (reversed): Points to the querant's fear of loss and the fear of losing financial security.

Card 4: **The Knight of Cups:** Indicates the influence of a young man of artistic ability who will bring new opportunities which will involve the querant.

Card 5: **Ace of Swords:** Those surrounding the querant possess mental clarity and intellectual focus. The querant will benefit from the positive influence of such people.

Card 6: **The Knight of Swords:** A strong assertive personality is indicated, who will assist the querant in any forthcoming difficulties. With a positive outlook, and determination, she will triumph over adversities.

Card 7: **Three of Cups:** This, the final card in the reading, points to great happiness and success for the querant. The card represents fulfilment and an abundance of good fortune. This card is an excellent indicator of a happy outcome for the querant in her new employment.

The Celtic Cross Spread

The **Celtic Cross** (see illustration on page 42) is perhaps the most common of all spreads, and certainly the most written about. For the beginner, however, it can be one of the most difficult to master. It consists of a total of ten cards, laid out in two separate steps; 1 - 6, then 7 - 10. Cards 1 - 6 are interpreted, then cards 7 - 10 which are read in turn.

The Celtic Cross is an excellent means to offer guidance on a specific problem, and the cards represent the following:

Card 1: **Current Influences**. Indicates the general direction of the reading.

Card 2: **Obstacles**. Indicates the immediate hurdles faced by the querant.

Card 3: **Specific Goals**. Querant's aims and desires, also the best which can be expected under present circumstances.

Card 4: **Past Foundations**. Points to distant past influences and actions which have resulted in a current situation.

Card 5: **Past Events**. This indicates influences from the recent past which are beginning to lose their impact.

Card 6: **Future Influences**. This indicates a new influence, as yet unknown to the querant but which will soon play an instrumental part in their life.

Card 7: **The Querant**. This provides further insight to the querant's attitude towards the current situation.

Card 8: **Home and Environment**. This offers insight into the part played by the querant in relation to their home and work environments and how he or she is perceived by others.

Card 9: **Inner Emotions**. Provides insight into querant's hopes and fears.

Card 10: **Final Outcome**. The final result, the consequence of all the influences revealed in the Celtic Cross Spread.

The Celtic Cross is especially useful in Tarot readings as it offers a great deal of background information, and therefore is much employed when the cards have to be laid out for a complete stranger.

Remember to emphasise any cards which belong to the Major Arcana, as they will play a more prominent part in the whole reading.

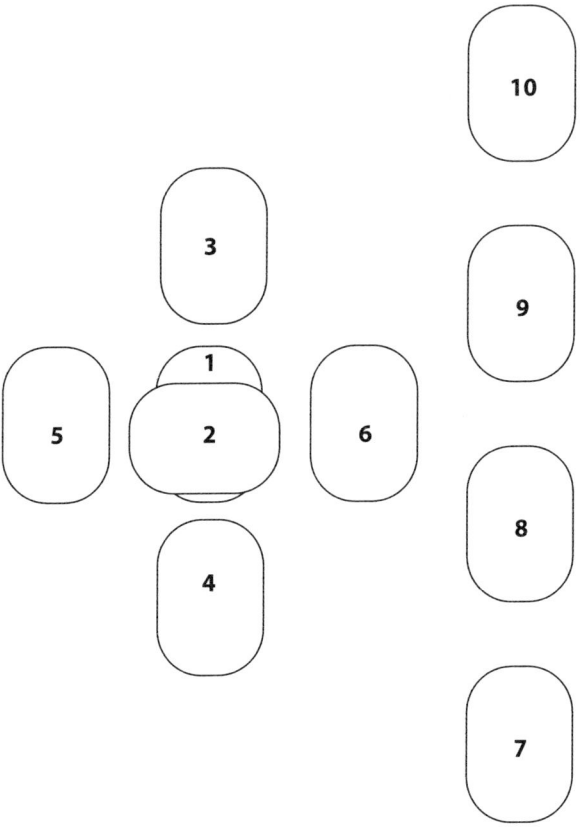

The Celtic Cross Spread

The Alchemist's Spread

Legend has it that the Alchemist's Spread dates back to the Middle Ages and was devised by Nostradamus. Therefore it is shrouded in mystery and should only be used once in each querant's lifetime. It relates to the querant's life as a whole, past, present and the final outcome which lies ahead, and should therefore be treated with extreme caution and sensitivity in a reading.

Six cards are shuffled as described above, and placed face down as illustrated. The cards are then interpreted thus:

Card 1: **The Past.** The whole of the querant's past life experiences.

Card 2: **The Present.** All the querant will achieve in their life.

Card 3: **The Future.** Where the querant will be at the end of their life.

Card 4: **Immediate Future Influences.** Influences on the querant's life in the immediate future.

Card 5: **Intermediate Future Influences.** Influences which will appear in the querant's life in the next few years.

Card 6: **Long-Term Future Influences.** Influences which will directly affect the final outcome of the querant's life.

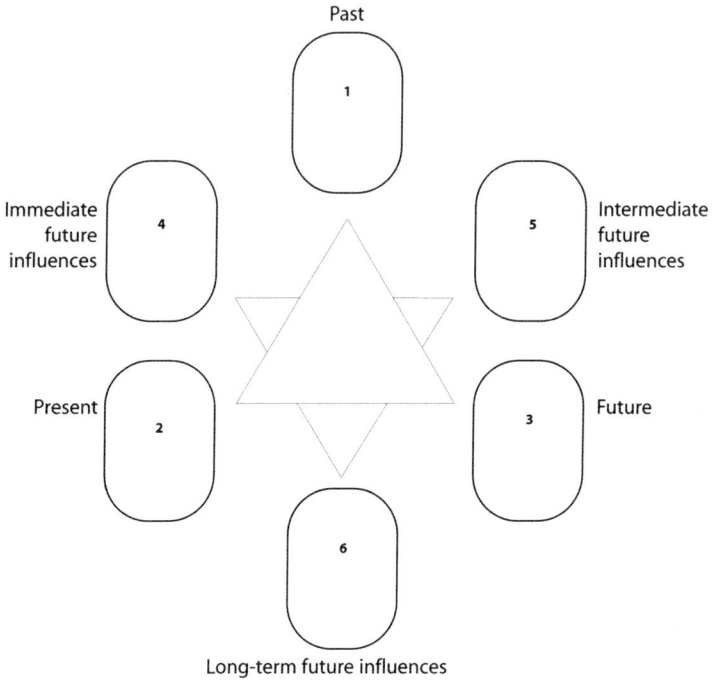

Past

1

Immediate future influences

4

Intermediate future influences

5

Present

2

Future

3

Long-term future influences

6

THE MAJOR ARCANA

The twenty-two cards of the Major Arcana contain a
wealth of symbolism and possible meanings. They are
considered the most important cards in the deck, and
each represent a fundamental aspect of the human
psyche. They are universally recognised images which
make references to astrology, classical myth and legend
or else Biblical imagery.

The word 'arcana' is plural for arcanum which means
'profound secret'. To the alchemists of the Middle Ages,
the arcanum was the secret of nature. The tarot cards
therefore are a body of secrets which can hold the key to
explaining our universe.

The twenty-two cards of the Major Arcana are at the
heart of the deck. Each card has a name and
corresponding number. Some cards are literal in
meaning such as 'Strength' whilst others are signify a
particular approach to life such as 'The Hermit' or 'The
Magician'. Astrological influences are represented by
'Moon', 'Sun' and 'Star'. They signify the elusive forces
associated with these heavenly bodies.

The cards of the Major Arcana draw out deep and
complex reactions in us. Many tarot readers view the
Major Arcana as showing the different stages in all our

lives. This is sometimes known as 'The Fool's Journey', ('The Fool' being the first card in the Major Arcana). The cards represent the qualities and experiences we must incorporate in our lives before we can realise our full potential, emotionally, spititually and physically.

On our journey, the twenty-two cards take us from our earliest awareness, 0 – 'The Fool', to fullfillment, 21 – 'The World'.

The cards are listed with their corresponding number below:

0	The Fool	11	Strength
1	The Magician	12	The Hanged Man
2	The High Priestess	13	Death
3	The Emperess	14	Temperance
4	The Emperor	15	The Devil
5	The Pope	16	The Tower
6	The Lovers	17	The Star
7	The Chariot	18	The Moon
8	Justice	19	The Sun
9	The Hermit	20	Judgement
10	The Wheel of Fortune	21	The World

In the following chapter, each card has assigned to it key words and certain meanings which are used in the art of Tarot divination. When the cards are placed upright they are considered dignified, and when viewed by the reader upside-down known as ill-dignified. For each card there is a general interpretation followed by a dignified and an ill-dignified meaning.

THE FOOL

THE FOOL
Beginning, spontaneity, optimism, major decisions

The Fool traditionally is either unnumbered or
occasionally is numbered zero. The image is of a man
dressed as a court jester. In Medievall times the jester
was held in high esteem in court and was frequently a
highly talented acrobat, singer or dancer.

By nature, the Fool was allowed to fly in the face of
convention and often satirised his masters and played
outrageous tricks which ordinary men dared not even
try.

To some, the Fool may be seen as disadvantaged
given that on the surface he seems to be naive as to the

ways of the world. However, reality in the Fool is one whose mind is not closed off to new and unusual experiences which would be denied by ordinary men.

The Fool symbolizes unpredictability, spontaneity, fun and surprises. He represents the untapped potential in all of us.

The Fool's philosophy can be seen as, 'It'll be all right in the end', and he has an unreserved passion for life and all its possibilities.

In tarot readings therefore the Fool can signify new beginnings, a new direction and the impetus to take a chance, no matter how irrational or crazy it may seem to others. The Fool urges to follow our instincts, act on our 'hunches' and take the path of adventure.

upright

If the card is upright it heralds new beginnings and a clean slate. It indicates unplanned and unexpected influences which will have a powerful effect on decisions and choices which have to be made. Depending on where the card is placed in the spread, that is, if it is surrounded by favourable cards, this card indicates perseverance will bring rewards, however, if it is surrounded by unfavourable cards, it urges the querant to be wary of pitfalls and to think matters through wisely before taking the next step. The Fool also indicates a specific type of person, an idealist, a visionary, one who can see further than the apparently obvious choice.

reversed

Thoughtlessness, lack of responsibility, immaturity
The Fool warns of major problems arising from
foolhardy and impetuous actions.

THE MAGICIAN

THE MAGICIAN
Action, potential, awareness, power

The Magician is assigned the number 1, the number of
determination, action and individuality. The Magician is
the archetypal masculine character, the ultimate
achiever. He grasps the situation and uses all
possibilities creatively, and can make them work for him.
His very stance as portrayed on the card shows him
acting as a lightning conductor. He extends one arm up
to the heavens for inspiration and points his other
toward the earth as a means of grounding this potent
energy. He is magical in that with his determination and
utter belief in his own abilities he can make what may

seem impossible actually happen. He has no qualms about putting his belief in himself on the line and will always act on it. He can identify and focus on a situation and turn it around to the best effect. This single-minded determination is how he gets incredible results.

upright

The Magician implies concentration and awareness. If you can focus on these qualities and know what you want, this card is the signal to believe in yourself and go and get it.

reversed

lack of self-confidence, indecision, deviousness
The Magician when placed upside down represents the abuse of power, treachery, and an inability to face reality.

THE HIGH PRIESTESS

THE HIGH PRIESTESS
Mystery, unconscious, awareness, understanding, wisdom

The High Priestess card has been assigned the number 2 which symbolises balance, relativity and the antithesis to the number one. She is the bridge between conscious and unconscious states, who can inspire dreams and visions which reveal the continuance of life beyond conscious boundaries.

The High Priestess is the protector of the unconscious. She is the feminine force which counteracts the masculine force of the Magician. Feminine archetypes in tarot are split between the High

Priestess and the Empress. The High Priestess, represents the mystery and inner wisdom of women. This card is also known in some decks as the Female Pope. She is certainly depicted in all variations of tarot as a wise woman dressed in gowns and wearing a crown similar to the hat of the Pope.

Legend has it that there was a female Pope who reigned successfully between 854-56. This legend of the Papess appeared in Europe around the end of the twelfth century and reached its peak in popularity at the time of the Reformation.

According to the legend, the Papess originally came from Mainz, in Germany. She fell in love with an Englishman and, masquerading as a young boy, travelled all over Europe with him eventually to Rome where she studied under the name Johannes Angelicus, where her brilliance was rewarded with the Papal office. Her brief reign came to an end when she died in childbirth whilst attending a solemn procession.

upright

The High Priestess challenges the querent to search deeper into their inner self, beyond the obvious, to tap into the vastness of their potential. The card symbolises the heart over the head. Depending where in the spread the High Priestess is placed, the card may indicate another person who will be able to assist the querant in making a decision. The High Priestess represents waiting and contemplation. It may not always be necessary to act to achieve your dreams and goals. They can come naturally through the course of time.

reversed

Lack of intuition, unrealised potential
If reversed, this card means the Querant must be wary of difficulties arising from emotional insecurity. If the querant is a man, this could signify the bad influence of a woman close to him on his life. It warns of the dangers faced if one fails to take sound advice or lacks intuition.

THE EMPRESS

THE EMPRESS
Nature, motherhood, realisation, senses

The Empress card has been assigned the number 3, the symbol of synthesis and harmony. The image on the card is one of a matronly woman seated outdoors. She signifies being at one with nature and is the source of all living things. The Empress represents birth, motherhood, new life and personal fulfilment. She urges us to never lose sight of our roots even though we can easily be swayed by superficial and material rewards. The Empress appeals to the senses, signifying pleasure, beauty and an abundance of well-being. She is the ultimate caring, sympathetic woman who lives life according to high moral standards and values. She is dedicated to the well-being of her family and has great insight into the problems faced by those close to her. The Empress as the mother figure is the first relationship the male querant has with a woman and can in many cases colour and influence subsequent relationships throughout his life. In extreme cases, this can become a negative aspect.

upright

This card when placed upright signifies, birth (not necessarily to the querant), fertility, pleasures of the senses and fulfilment. Domestic harmony and maternal care and protection are present, representing roots and a firm foundation for future progress. An involvement with nature offers inspiration and reassurance, as does artistic creativity.

reversed

Domestic upheaval, missed opportunities
Emotional discord in the home, overpowering maternal forces, infertility, unwanted pregnancy, insecurity, conflicts between the sexes, suppressed artistic expression.

THE EMPEROR

THE EMPEROR
Authority, protection, discipline, provider

The Emperor is allocated number 4 symbolising
organisation, reason and willpower. He is the partner of
the Empress but represents power over love. The
Emperor is depicted seated poker-straight on a throne,
his gaze meeting ours directly and signifies absolute
control and self-confidence.

The Emperor lives in a world where rules are
followed, logic and reason are paramount. He can
symbolise a figure of authority, a leader which could be
the querant or a person or institution known to them.
He relies on tangible facts and his methodical approach

makes him the focus of much admiration from those around him. He is the archetypal father, he provides, guides and protects us. His heavy crown symbolises his worldly authority, yet he is surrounded by barren land in direct contrast to his mate the Empress, which suggests the sterility of the masculine world founded purely on power over the 'feminine' attributes of beauty and nature.

Just as the male child's first female experience is with his mother, The Empress, so the female child sees her father as The Emperor. The paternal image is one which stays with the woman her entire life. They can live their lives doing what they believe their father would have wanted and can often lose sight of their own opinions and direction believing their father's opinion much more valuable or sensible than their own. This need not always be a negative trait, however, and can signify powerful traditionally 'masculine' qualities in a woman such as determination, strength of will, courage and nerves of steel. In this case the Emperor is on the one hand an unrelenting, overpowering tyrant, and on the other a mighty ally.

upright

The Emperor signifies a strong-willed character who has gained knowledge through a wealth of experiences. He possesses self-control, authority and ambition. A powerful ally with much influence and wisdom at the disposal of the querant.

reversed

Weakness, failed ambition
Insecurity around a figure in authority be it a father or a boss for example, failure to realise ambition, immaturity.

THE HIEROPHANT

THE POPE
The pursuit of knowledge, conformity, group
identification, faith

Also known as The Hierophant, we see the Pope dressed
in the elaborate robes of office seated between two
pillars. Kneeling at his feet are two priests who he
welcomes into the church. This symbolism is not merely
representative of religious institutions, but more of a
wish to pursue knowledge through a structured group
environment be it university, school, a society, company
or club. The emphasis is on group identity as opposed
to the individual, and adhering to rules, discipline,
rituals and procedures.

The Pope represents the value of such institutions. In many ways he is the opposite of the Fool. He points to conformity, traditional values and the necessity to do what is expected. He likes his world to be rational, ordered and carefully labelled and views those of us who muddle along with disdain. He believes the methods correct for him are therefore correct for everyone else. His philosophy for life may contain much that is good and progressive, but he can lack empathy, humanity and spontaneity.

upright

Good counsel, a giver of knowledge and enlightenment. The value of moral, educational or social convention. The importance of group identity, loyalty to others as part of a team. Freedom through knowledge.

reversed

Misinformation, devious practices
Distortion of the truth, bad advice, overbearing individual, slander.

THE LOVERS

THE LOVERS
Desire, conflicting choices, relationships

This card relates to intimate relationships, forming bonds with others, physical attraction towards another, struggling with temptation and establishing what or who you really care about.

The Lovers in short refer to love and sex. The basic human condition drives us toward the need for union with another. This emotion is incredibly powerful and can be all-encompassing. The angel (cupid) above offers his blessing toward The Lovers and represents deep love, the strongest force of all. This relationship need not be sexual: more generally The Lovers can point to the force that draws any two entities together be it people, ideas, events or groups.

It is also the card of tough decision as symbolised by the man standing between two women, one representing the temptress, the other the virgin. (Reminiscent of Adam and Eve). This is symbolic of the need to overcome temptation when at a crossroads in our lives. This card signals only a firm belief in yourself and your values will take you on the correct path, even though there may be forces around you urging you to follow the wrong one.

upright

Upright, this card represents a time of choice, of a major dilemma where the outcome will be of paramount importance. If The Lovers appear in your spread, it indicates relying on your heart over your head, inspiration over reason for the correct way forward. You must draw on your maturity and integrity and not be swayed by temptations which may be in the guise of the 'easier option'.

reversed

Moral lapse, temptation, indecision
The Lovers reversed signals severe temptation will be placed in the querant's path. Be warned of not staying true to your morals and values. Do not try to 'have your

cake and eat it', this will only affect your judgement and
ultimately will be to your loss.

THE CHARIOT

THE CHARIOT
Triumph, self-belief, assertiveness, control

The Chariot has been allocated the number 7 in the deck, seven being the number of progress, self-expression and independent action.

This card represents the fulfilling of goals, success, determination and letting nothing stand in your way. The Chariot indicates leading from the front, and coming out on top, victorious.

Imagine Julius Caesar riding victorious into Rome, after defeating his enemies and conquering new lands. The Chariot symbolises the fact all victories are possible through willpower, self-belief, determination and concentration. All is possible if you can remain focused and always have a clear vision of what you want and how to get it.

The military imagery of The Chariot is appropriate as discipline, guts, steely will power and assertiveness are imperative qualities in the quest to achieve your goals.

This card represents the ego, not the showy side, but the positive aspects of being self assured and confident.

upright

Upright, The Chariot points to success, triumph over adversity, victory achieved through concentrated effort, having complete belief in yourself and your abilities - you are the key to your success.

reversed

Overbearing, inflated ego
If the Chariot is reversed, it points to ruthlessness. Beware of one who would trample over anyone or anything standing in their way. There is a danger of egocentricity and inattention to the rights of others.

JUSTICE

JUSTICE
Arbitration, truth, integrity

This card depicts a stern woman seated holding the scales of equality and impartial judgement in one hand and the sword of decision in the other. The card has been allocated the number 8, the number of Justice as used by the Greeks as it is made up of equal divisions of equal numbers suggesting balance and equanimity.

It relates to fairness, legal concerns, honesty, accountability and acknowledging the truth, accepting responsibility for your actions.

In a reading, the Justice card infers that life is ultimately just and fair. We may think, with good reason, this is not the case, but Justice reminds us there is divine balance.

Justice certainly represents legal matters, yet is not confined to the courtroom. In readings, this card can appear when you are concerned you are doing the right thing, or are aware of the possible consequences of an action or decision.

Justice urges us to take our responsibilities seriously, to face facts and recognise our mistakes. We must carefully weigh up all the facts and possibilities before coming to a decision.

upright

If the card is upright, it points to agreements and decisions based on negotiation and careful weighing up of facts; the vindication of truth and honour; of facing up to responsibilities and being accountable for our actions, maturity and strength of character.

reversed

Prejudice, bias, injustice
If the card is reversed, it warns of injustice, of prejudice and lack of fair play. In legal matters, it can warn of miscarriages of justice and the feeling the law is not on your side after all.

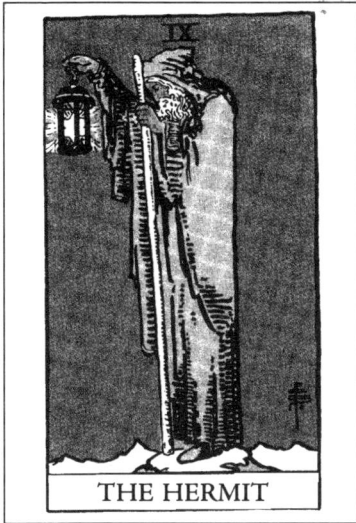

THE HERMIT

THE HERMIT
Introspection, seeking, guidance, solitude

The Hermit is card number 9 in the tarot sequence.
Nine is important symbolically in that it is the last of the
single numbers; after it we return to number one, or
unity, therefore this card signifies the end of the first half
of the Major Arcana.

The illustration on this card depicts an old man
wrapped in long robes reminiscent of a monk, he
clutches a staff and holds a lamp in front to guide him
on his way. This imagery relates to Diogenes, the Greek
ascetic, who, legend has it, went out with a lantern on a
quest to find an honest man. He symbolises the search

for truth and the discarding of all distractions.

In readings, The Hermit suggests a need for solitude, to give yourself time to reflect, for quiet contemplation. We are told, 'Seek and ye shall find', this card signifies guidance; we learn as we develop, from parents and teachers amongst others, and, of course, from experience, and in turn we pass on our knowledge as we progress through our lives. This card represents a time in our lives when we may question the obvious, when we sense there is a deeper reality and search for it. This is a solitary quest, as the answer is not in the external, material world, but deep within ourselves.

upright

Upright, the card points to careful planning and contemplation before making a decision. It urges the Querant to take a 'back seat' to retire from the hustle and bustle of everyday life to think and plan. Take advice from someone you trust, whose advice you believe to be sound. Take as long as you need before progressing further.

reversed

Obstinacy, suspicion, refusal to take good advice
When reversed, this card can signify obstinacy, the refusal to take sound advice, relying on yourself even when you know assistance would be beneficial. The card

warns against unfounded suspicions regarding others' motives and a fear of progress and innovation.

WHEEL OF FORTUNE

THE WHEEL OF FORTUNE
Destiny, turning points, movement, vision

This is number 10 of the Major Arcana. This is the first of the second half of the sequence and symbolises new beginnings. Traditionally, ten is thought of as a perfect number and therefore the symbol of perfection is the circle or wheel.

The Wheel of Fortune represents chance, finding opportunity, a change of fortune. It is generally to be interpreted as an optimistic card, signifying greater perspective for even though we set out and plan our own life path, we are subject to greater forces and influences which affect our lives. We all experience what seem to be coincidences or chance situations which are in actual fact all part of the great plan. How often has a chance encounter become a major player in our life, be it, for example, romantic or career orientated?

The card signifies the unexpected twists of fate. The action of the wheel itself is indicated - when the energy of the wheel arrives in your life, events will accelerate. As the saying goes, "round and round and round she goes, where she stops, nobody knows."

In readings, The Wheel can indicate vision or realisation will strike with unprecedented force. If the querant is experiencing a problem or is unable to resolve a dilemma, The Wheel advises standing back and viewing the issue from a wider perspective. This may sound as if circumstances are outwith the querant's control, however the changes or results will at the end of the day be positive.

upright

Upright, The Wheel of Fortune signals a new cycle in the querant's affairs. We rely on the forces of fate and destiny, over which we have no control, yet we can rest assured this ultimately will bring true rewards.

reversed

Reversal of fortune, unforeseen obstacles
When reversed, it signifies a turn for the worse, a

reversal of fortune. It indicates a negative phase in the querant's life. These adversities will have to be endured until the wheel has revolved full circle in the fullness of time.

STRENGTH

STRENGTH
Strength, patience, compassion, gentle control

Also known in some decks as 'Fortitude', Strength depicts a young woman guiding a lion (itself a symbol of power and strength) using nothing but her hands and gentle expression.

Strength is card 11 and this number is traditionally associated with vulnerability, danger and the need to reconcile divergent qualities.

The card relates to endurance, unshakeable resolve, accepting and mediating between conflicting forces, forgiving and being gently influential to others and demonstrating empathy. The card urges us to draw on our inner strength, even in times when it would be easier to lose our temper, and to try and understand others who try our patience. Strength encourages us to adapt a 'softly-softly' approach toward situations and not exert the authority and mastery of The Chariot.

In a reading, Strength urges us not to give up, to rely on our inner resources of compassion and patience. If others are pushing you to the limit, it is better to concentrate on the strength which comes through love and forbearance. This will see you through even in your darkest moments.

upright

When upright, Strength urges the querant to channel negative impulses such as envy, impatience and spite and turn them into positive energy in order to triumph over adversity. If you can do this, your rewards will be all the richer.

reversed

Lack of self-control, defeat, loss of opportunity
When reversed, the card can indicate failure if the querant surrenders to negative forces. This can result in missed opportunities and a lack of self-discipline.

THE HANGED MAN

THE HANGED MAN
Transition, reversal, suspension, martyrdom

This is certainly one of the most disturbing images in tarot. We see a young man, suspended by his right foot, his hands bound behind his back, yet his face has an expression of calm detachment, of acceptance. His head is surrounded by a halo, which indicates divine understanding. He has sacrificed himself, yet he has still won.

The number 12 is allocated to The Hanged Man. In Arabic numerals it is a combination of the numbers one and two - signifying the interaction of unity with duality which in turn, creates the third dimension. The traumas of number eleven are over, and therefore The Hanged Man is not a card to be feared, as it is a symbol of rebirth and deliverance.

The Hanged Man represents emotional release, acceptance and surrendering to experience. It is also associated with putting your faith in others, and suspending the need to act, preferring to wait for the ideal opportunity to come along.

This card urges us to know when to let go, when to surrender in order to emerge triumphant. Take time, stand still. When we stand still, we suspend time, hence we have all the time in the world.

In readings, The Hanged Man points to the fact that the most obvious answer to a problem is not necessarily the correct one. The card is full of contradictions; if we wish to force our will on another, we must instead let go; if we desperately want something our own way, sacrifice to the will of another and when we have a fierce urge to act, then wait. Ironically, if we make these contradictory moves, then we will find the answer to our question.

upright

When upright, the card points to an ability to adapt to changing circumstances, to be willing to accept others' will and to make sacrifices whether they be material or emotional. By doing this, a new sense of emotional fulfilment will be yours.

reversed

Materialism, inability to accept reality
When reversed, The Hanged Man warns of the pitfalls of sacrificing one's spiritual and emotional needs in favour of material and egotistical goals. A weakness of will and being easily led is indicated as is a lack of direction. This ultimately will lead to missed opportunities and stagnation.

DEATH

DEATH
Endings, transition, clearance, inexorable forces

The Death card is arguably, especially in the case of the new querant, the most disturbing image in the entire deck. The dark skeletal figure of card 13 is representative of our deepest fear: the unknown. The number 13 itself symbolises death and has unfortunate superstitious connotations even today. The appearance of the Grim Reaper beneath the number 13 seems highly appropriate. On the card we see this animated skeleton brandishing a large scythe. He is mowing a field of black earth, yet his crop is not wheat or corn, but dismembered human bodies .

When the Death card appears in a spread, it would be fair to say the querant should be alarmed, yet this card does not indicate permanent end but a closing of doors and a new chapter in life. Death in tarot means to grow, to develop and to do this we must first 'die' in order to leave the old life and embrace the new.

Simply, the Death card symbolises the end of an era, putting the past behind and shedding the trappings of the old life. This can be a frightening prospect, moving from the known to the unknown, but to succeed we must at times face the unavoidable.

In readings, card 13 represents a huge life change, i.e a change of a relationship, a change in career. This will most probably be accompanied by feelings of sadness, grief, loss and fear of the unknown. A sense of relief and the need to get rid of all the trappings of the past are indicated. The Death card urges us to do away with all unnecessary "baggage" and get down to the bare bones of what is really important. Just as Death is inevitable, so is change.

upright

When upright the Death card signifies unprecedented change in circumstances. These changes may seem cataclysmic at the time but will turn out to be a blessing in disguise. They will make way for a better way forward. When change occurs, the best approach is to embrace it and put your trust in the outcome. It points to clearing away the old and making way for the new.

reversed

Stagnation, lost opportunity
The card, when reversed, is an indication that the querant is resisting necessary change. Death signifies that a refusal to face reality will result in missed opportunity and stagnation.

TEMPERANCE

TEMPERANCE
Moderation, compromise, harmony, health

Temperance is shown as a winged figure standing
outdoors pouring water from a pitcher held in her right
hand to the one in her left. The word 'Temperance' in
this context means to combine ingredients to the correct
proportions thus creating harmony and balance.

The card is number 14 in the Major Arcana. In
Arabic numerals, this number is made up of one and
four; the combination of unity and the quaternary
produces the pentagon, the five-sided shape symbolic of
growth, inspiration and the combination of several
elements to create the greater whole.

The card is one of quiet deliberation, display moderation and self-restraint. Temperance indicates a need for balance. In situations of conflict, the Temperance card points to the need for compromise and the ability to understand both sides of the argument. It is also the card of good health on all levels, spiritual, physical and emotional.

upright

When viewed upright, this card indicates success can be achieved through careful harnessing of volatile forces. By carefully combining all factors and recognising all sides, progress can be made.

reversed

Impatience, lack of foresight
Reversed, this card warns of the dangers of self-indulgence and an inability to find direction. Lack of foresight and necessary contemplation can lead to clumsy decision making and therefore progress will be thwarted. Do not give in to impatience and rash decisions however frustrated you may feel. This card also signifies potential conflicts in relationships both personal and business.

THE DEVIL

THE DEVIL
Futility, trappings, ignorance, anger

The Devil is the universal symbol of everything that we
deem evil and undesirable in our lives. The image is one
of a sinister winged figure standing on a stone plinth. At
his feet stand two lesser demons both with chains
around their necks which are fixed to the Devil's plinth.

The card number is 15, which in Arabic numbers
reduces to six. Six is the number of the combination of
opposite principles and is the number of Love. The six-
pointed star or hexagram is made up of two intertwined
triangles: the upward pointing alchemical symbol of fire
combined with the downward-pointing symbol of water.

Therefore, we have another card which is concerned with the synthesis of consciousness with unconscious elements.

Throughout our lives, we see good and bad as light and dark. In order to do good, we must first banish the dark. The truth is that darkness is merely the absence of light which in a spiritual sense means the presence of errors which hide the truth. The Devil symbolises these errors.

The Devil warns against ignorance, being in the dark and not realising we are there. It points to materialism and the obsession with superficial trappings as opposed to what is really important and it represents futility, the lack of belief in ourselves and where we are going.

The Devil is universally feared as the embodiment of evil, but in Tarot fortunately has no such worrying connotations.

upright

When viewed upright, this card points to unhealthy, unproductive situations. It warns against burying our heads in the sand and refusing to face the truth, no matter how painful it may be. In the case of relationships, the Devil card indicates there could be a person you are obsessed with or who exerts too much influence over you who you follow even though you know in your heart of hearts they are no good for you. In this case, the Devil prompts you to examine the situation realistically, considering all the facts.

The Devil card when viewed upright relates to entrapment. The querant may be in a situation where he or she sees no possible escape or is beholden to a person who is no good for them.

reversed

Abuse of position, frustration, lust for power
When reversed, the Devil warns against surrendering to frustration and feelings of futility. Do not give in to the temptation to abuse your position or vent anger on others who are in no way to blame for your situation.

THE TOWER

THE TOWER
Downfall, sweeping, sudden change, re-evaluation

The Tower is depicted as a sturdy building set on a hill which has been struck by a bolt of lightning. Such is the force of its power that the castellated top of the tower has been severed from the rest of the building, flames soar toward the sky and two stricken figures plunge headlong to certain death.

The Tower is number 16. In Arabic numerals, this is made up from one and six, which reduce to seven. Seven is a solar number signifying power and positive action.

The imagery of the card itself is unsettling. The appearance in a spread does not bode well for one who likes predictability, routine and is content with their lot. This card represents sudden and dramatic life changes, not gradual, planned transition.

The Tower signifies the catalysts in our lives; the dramatic, often terrifying experiences which force us to wake up and face up to reality, to respond to a situation. Something's wrong, and for some reason, you are not responding. Is it you that are too proud? If so, then expect a blow to your ego. Are you suppressing your true feelings on a subject? Prepare for an emotional outburst. Do you feel you are stuck in a rut and are going nowhere? Expect a huge surprise which could alter the course of your life.

This card is the embodiment of disruption, upheaval, chaos, sudden realisation and emotional outbursts. This may sound rather intimidating, and it is up to you how you choose to interpret and respond to the Tower's influence.

upright

When viewed upright, the Tower encourages the querant to recognise the fact that disruption and sweeping change can be put to positive effect because it is needed to push our lives along to the next stage. Upheaval can be used to force a new direction which you never dreamed was possible. Seize the opportunity and use the change positively as a basis for a new beginning.

reversed

Unnecessary suffering, self-undoing
The reversed Tower indicates unnecessary suffering. In this situation, change may have been more apparent, hence the accompanying disruption and possible misery might have been avoided.

THE STAR

THE STAR
Hope, serenity, generosity, inspiration

When we gaze at the stars for inspiration, we feel our problems are tiny in comparison with the vast, twinkling eternity of the night sky.

On the card, a naked girl is seen kneeling by a stream pouring water from two pitchers. Above, eight stars are visible, with one being distinctive in its greater size and more pronounced shape.

The card is number 17, which, in Arabic numerals, reduces to eight. Because of its shape, the number eight symbolised renewal and rebirth. Also, the eighth sphere of the firmament was thought to be occupied by the fixed stars.

The Star is one of the most welcome cards in any spread, particularly if the querant has recently suffered periods of sadness or grief. The card indicates there is light at the end of the tunnel, and reminds us to have and keep our faith that all will be well in the end. In this sense, it is the direct opposite of the Devil card which makes us doubt our own abilities and scoffs at hope for the future.

The Star also urges us to stop holding back, to open our hearts and minds, and release our fears and doubts. This card, however, is not one of practical solutions, but more of the need to hang on to hope and to keep the faith. When card 17 appears in a spread, use it to know you are on the right track. When you are on your journey, remember to use the light of the Star to guide you and never lose sight of it, for all will be well in the end.

upright

When viewed upright, the Star indicates insight into future possibilities, which will bring happiness and fulfilment. A tranquil period is highlighted, and this is particularly positive where the querant is recovering from an illness, bereavement or any emotional upheaval. A widening of horizons is indicated, as is a new zest for life which allows you to flourish.

reversed

Self-doubt, lack of trust
When reversed, the Star warns of the dangers of closing your mind to new possibilities. This will result in a lack of progress. It can also indicate a lack of trust and the misery of self-doubt.

THE MOON

THE MOON
Fear, illusion, imagination, bewilderment

The card depicts a deep, mysterious pool from which a crayfish is struggling to crawl. There are two dogs guarding the pool, both have their heads raised to the moon above. In the distance, there are two imposing towers which represent the gateway to the unknown and mystical regions beyond.

This card is numbered 18 in the sequence. In Arabic numbers this is reduced to nine, nine being the final part of another stage of the quest. This card like the number nine card of the Hermit, symbolises solitude and vulnerability.

The Moon represents the world outside our normal, environment, the mysterious universe waiting outside our everyday experiences. We may, on the whole, choose to ignore what we feel we cannot understand, and only take a peek from time to time through our imagination, or be thrust into a new world, through drugs, madness, or intense experiences such as death, battle or grief, which terrifies us when we are unprepared and disorientated.

upright

This may sound a little frightening when viewed upright, but positive aspects of the Moon point to the fact that letting a little of the mysterious into our everyday lives is not necessarily a bad thing. Do not be afraid to imagine all you desire can be yours for the moon guides us and shows us how we can be open to new and unexpected possibilities in our lives.

reversed

Lack of nerve, confusion, unrealistic goals
However, when viewed in reverse, the Moon also stands for our deep-rooted fears and anxieties. When we wake up in the middle of the night, our problems seem much more insurmountable by the light of the moon. We cannot find our way so easily in the moonlight. In this sense the Moon indicates being lost and aimless. Take

care to follow the truth and not be carried away chasing impossible dreams and unrealistic goals, you are only deceiving yourself. The Moon reversed also points to a failure of nerve and a fear of stepping beyond what we know are safe boundaries, this will lead to missed opportunities.

THE SUN

THE SUN
Enlightenment, vitality, greatness, confidence

The Sun card depicts one child standing or dancing by a wall. The sun hangs resplendent high in the sky and drops of liquid fall from its rays.

The card is number 19 and in Arabic numerals reduces to ten. Ten is a return to unity and like card ten, The Wheel of Fortune, suggests the protective qualities of the circle or sphere. The children are shown in many decks to be standing on a circular pool of light, or a magic circle, which protects them from danger and is a place which they can bask in the light and warmth of the sun and, like all living things, n grow and flourish.

The Sun card literally reflects the power and the glory of light. When any light appears it illuminates our world, be it when the sun comes up in the morning, and chases all the shadows and nightmares away, or simply when a lamp is clicked on in a room illuminating every corner. We claim to 'have seen the light' when realisation hits us, when we feel we have been wandering around blind to the obvious.

Throughout history, people from many cultures have worshipped the sun as a giver of light and warmth. The Sun symbolises vigour, courage, radiance and is the central force which makes everything in life possible.

upright

When viewed upright, the Sun urges the querant to have complete and utter belief in themselves. Be sure of your qualities and abilities on every level. Your energy knows no limits and you radiate self-confidence, good health and well-being. You stand out from the crowd and are admired and revered by all around you. This is not about egos, but about knowing and believing in who you are, and having the confidence to become successful at all you choose to undertake. When you see this card use it to let your light shine.

reversed

Misjudgement, potential failure
The Sun in reverse can warn of the dangers of misjudgement, of unrealistic goals which could be the result of an inflated ego. Beware fantasies replacing real success.

THE JUDGEMENT

JUDGEMENT
Rebirth, absolution, decisions

A winged angel, blowing a trumpet looks down from the sky. Below, gazing up in response are three naked figures (a man, woman and child). The card depicts the scene of the Last Judgement, when an archangel shall blow the last trump and the dead rise from their graves, when all who have lived good and honest lives on earth shall gain entry into heaven.

However, what is the fate of those who have sinned? Will they be denied access? This is the element of Judgement we find unsettling. How can Judgement be reconciled with forgiveness?

The card is number twenty in the tarot sequence, and this symbolises the duality of the number two, however this time there is less opposition between higher and lower planes. They are working more closely together as we reach the end of the tarot sequence of the Major Arcana. This point is evident as the figures on the card are the fully grown man and woman, with the child of their union. They have grown, matured, progressed and the child is a symbol of potential realised, of new life and rebirth.

Judgement in a reading urges the querant to move away from the belief that if you (or others) have committed a sin then you are ultimately a 'bad person'. It is possible to judge without condemning. Assess all the facts, consider all sides to find the truth.

Card twenty reminds us that at times we must decide, that however difficult this may be, we have to make that decision. By referring to the message in the Judgement card, we examine the facts, consider and decide with a clear conscience. Even if we are the ones being judged, we must turn this into a positive experience and learn from it.

Judgement urges us to put the mistakes of the past behind us. Be ready and willing to start afresh. With this atonement for past mistakes we can move on and feel cleansed, and in a sense, reborn. This feeling of absolution can push us toward a specific path, very often one which we dared not follow previously.

This card holds particular relevance if the querant is going through a difficult stage in his or her life. Seeing the Judgement card in a spread encourages us to remember that a new chapter, a new beginning, is not too far away.

upright

Upright, the Judgement card signifies accomplishment and the accompanying pleasure experienced when efforts have deservedly been rewarded. A return to good health is indicated as is a new lease of life. A bright future beckons.

reversed

Guilt, loss, self-reproach
Reversed, Judgement also signifies change, however here it is linked with self-reproach and guilt over wasted opportunities and a sense of under- achievement. This is when the mistakes of the past still haunt, and blur the way forward.

THE WORLD

THE WORLD
Fulfilment, completion, wholeness, satisfaction

The World card depicts a young girl figure dancing in the centre of an encircling wreath. She carries a wand in each hand and the only garment she wears is a loose veil. The wreath is the symbol of completion, of the ultimate victory.

This is the final card in the sequence and is numbered 21. In Arabic numbers, this reduces to three, which is the number of synthesis and creation.

The World represents fulfilment, and a deep appreciation for what you have in your personal life. This feeling can come at any time, be it sitting at home with your family, or winning a gold medal. It can take the form of a wonderful, warm sensation or an overpowering and joyful outburst. This card helps us to find out where this feeling comes from.

We feel happiest when every facet of our lives is working together, when we really feel we are moving toward our dreams and goals.

In readings, the World represents these feelings of fulfilment, of being blessed, and is the most powerful card in the deck, signifying you are now in the position to pursue and ultimately achieve everything you truly want.

upright

Upright, the World signifies the final and successful outcome of a venture. It is the card of potential fulfilled, of satisfaction, of efforts rewarded. It is the culmination of events, of happy outcomes and indicates material wealth and greater spiritual awareness.

reversed

Stagnation, lack of will
Reversed, this card warns of waiting for the world to come to you. This can result in a loss of momentum, impatience, delays, and stagnation.

THE MINOR ARCANA

The Minor Arcana consists of 56 cards, which are very different in form to those of the Major Arcana.

In Tarot, the Major Arcana supplies the universal themes, the direction, and the leading emphases in a reading. These are harnessed by the cards of the Minor Arcana and brought down to a practical level which can be interpreted, related and acted upon in the course of daily life. The cards of the Minor Arcana represent the emotions, concerns and activities which make up all our lives.

The Minor Arcana is made up of four suits of fourteen cards which are similar in structure to normal playing cards. These suits can be tied to four elements of Fire, Water, Earth and Air. The following will provide a good basic understanding of the meanings behind the four suits of the Minor Arcana and so help interpretation.

Wands

Wands are the symbol of action, creativity, and movement. They represent a love of life, fearlessness and self-confidence, the launching of new schemes and ideas

Parsed 0 of 0 0

and positive action. Wands are linked with the Fire
element, hence, astrologically they are associated with
the fire signs of Aries, Leo and Sagittarius. In a negative
sense, they can represent reckless behaviour and
subsequent disappointment.

Cups

Cups symbolise spiritual and emotional experience.
They are associated with the Water element, and the
corresponding astrological signs of Pisces, Cancer and
Scorpio and relate to dreams, peace and fulfilment. In a
negative sense they can indicate an inability to face up to
reality, unrealistic expectations and over-sensitivity.

Swords

This is the suit of intellect, thought and reason. Swords
represent mental clarity, justice and truth. Swords are
associated with the Air element and the corresponding
astrological signs of Gemini, Libra and Aquarius. In a
negative sense, they are associated with severing ties,
often causing emotional disharmony and unhappiness.

Pentacles

This is the suit of practicality, security and material
concerns. Pentacles stand for the tangible, physical
world, and working toward positive results. They are
associated with the Earth element and corresponding
astrological signs of Taurus, Virgo and Capricorn, and
display an enjoyment of the physical world. In a

negative sense, they can indicate greed, and superficial pleasures.

The suits are also associated with the Chinese philosophy of Yin and Yang. Swords and Wands form the Yang, masculine principle and Pentacles and Cups the Yin, feminine principle.

Each suit of the Minor Arcana contains four court cards: King, Queen, Knight and Page, and ten other cards numbered from ace to ten. It is the court cards we will study first. These cards are not representative of circumstances but of people. When a court card appears in a reading, it signifies a particular person whose influence will affect future decisions and actions.

Logically, when the court cards are upright, they represent a positive, helpful individual, and when reversed, warn of potential treachery and rejection.

The characteristics associated with each court card are as follows:

Wands		
CARD	AGE	APPEARANCE
King	Male 35+	Red/Fair hair Hazel/Grey eyes
Queen	Female 35+	Red/Fair hair Brown/Blue eyes
Knight	Male under 35	Fair hair Grey/Blue eyes
Page	Boy/girl	Red/Fair hair Blue/Green eyes

Cups

CARD	AGE	APPEARANCE
King	Male 35+	Fair hair Blue eyes
Queen	Female 35+	Brown/fair hair Blue eyes
Knight	Male under 35	Brown hair Blue/Grey eyes
Page	Boy/girl	Brown hair Blue/Brown eyes

Swords

CARD	AGE	APPEARANCE
King	Male 35+	Dark Brown/Black hair, Dark eyes
Queen	Female 35+	Light Brown hair Gray eyes
Knight	Male under 35	Dark Brown hair, Dark eyes
Page	Boy/girl	Light Brown hair, Blue eyes

Pentacles		
CARD	AGE	APPEARANCE
King	Male 35+	Dark Brown/Black hair, Dark eyes
Queen	Female 35+	Black/dark Brown hair, Dark eyes
Knight	Male under 35	Brown hair, Dark eyes
Page	Boy/girl	Brown hair Dark eyes

The following chapter will explain the meaning dignified and ill-dignified, for each of the 56 cards of the Minor Arcana. These meanings are according to those devised by the Order of the Golden Dawn and are universally used by Tarot readers. Although of relatively recent origin, the interpretations allocated to each card have been proven to cover practically any life situation be it career, health, relationships or wealth.

THE SUIT OF WANDS
Career, enterprise, creativity, ambition

This suit is associated with the world of work, career and ambition. As mentioned earlier, the suit of Wands is linked with the element Fire, therefore it is no surprise that the characteristics attributed to the star signs of Leo, Aries and Sagittarius, of fiery determination, creativity, enthusiasm, and energy, are predominant in this suit.

A predominance of Wands in a reading will therefore relate to career matters, and can be especially informative for anyone who is planning or undertaking a new enterprise. The presence of Coins alongside the Wands in the spread will also have added significance, indicating possible financial outcomes. However, do not despair if there is a lack of Coins in the reading, this could merely indicate that financial reward is perhaps not of paramount importance, will be further in the future than anticipated, or is not of a material nature, not that the venture will fail.

Wands in a reading certainly point to the fact that whatever the future may hold, it will be met head-on with enthusiasm, determination and passion.

ACE OF WANDS

ACE OF WANDS
Creativity, originality, new beginnings, fertility

upright

Upright, this card relates to fresh starts, new enterprises and challenges. These are generally linked to career matters, however, it can also signify the birth of a child depending on how the card relates to others in a reading. Whatever the point of focus in the querant's life, the Ace of Wands indicates the task in hand will be undertaken with creativity, inspiration, inventiveness and enthusiasm.

Frustration, greed, overconfidence
Reversed, this card warns of the dangers of unrealistic
expectations and an inflated ego and the frustrations
and disappointments which can result. It can also
indicate impotence and sterility.

TWO OF WANDS
Earned success, partnership, self-doubt

<u>upright</u>

The Two of Wands signifies strength of will bringing success to ventures, and a sense of achievement through just means and hard work (can indicate promotion, successful business venture, financial security). This card also suggests partnership, the meeting of ideas, which will ultimately be positive for the querant and wisdom gained through experience, and the responsible wielding of executive powers. However, also associated with this card are feelings of anxiety, a fear of the future, and worry that everything could just fall apart.

reversed

Pride without humility, futility, worthless goals
Reversed, this card points to problems particularly with colleagues and partners at work. The Two of Wands also signifies wealth and success attained by dishonourable means, over-ambition and pride without humility. The negative aspects of the dignified meaning attributed to this card begins to dominate; when the querant will suffer from self-doubt and loss of faith in their motives. Success will seem worthless.

THREE OF WANDS
New ventures, conviction, partnerships

upright

This card signifies the successful launching of a new venture or enterprise. This is when original ideas are put into action. This card indicates an extremely productive period in the querant's life and should be a welcome sight in a reading particularly if there are projects and plans requiring conviction, inventiveness and sheer effort. The card suggests success will not be immediate, but to keep going, as it is assured in the longterm. The card points to a complementary partnership: the thinker (ideas, vision) and the 'doer' (practical skills, logic, common-sense and knowledge).

reversed

Failure of nerve, frustration, personality clashes
Reversed, this card indicates an inability to communicate ideas and separate imagination from reality, consequently resulting in missed opportunities and wasted talents. The frustrations of reality can cause impatience and a retreat into a fantasy world where grand schemes and plans come to nothing. Pride and obstinacy result in a refusal to accept help and assistance, and personality clashes are indicated with a partner.

FOUR OF WANDS
Satisfaction, completion, new-home

upright

Upright, this card signifies the successful conclusion of a
venture or relationship and the wonderful feelings of
satisfaction and joy which follow. The Four of Wands is
associated with new beginnings particularly when
related to the home, hence moving house is indicated,
however, depending on the surrounding cards in a
reading, this can also signify the beginning of a new
relationship or romance.

reversed

Decadence, snobbishness, impatience
When reversed, this card signifies that the positive
completion of an idea or venture as mentioned above
will not be as quick to arrive as desired. This,
fortunately, does not mean that it is a straight reversal of
the happy conclusion indicated in the upright Four of
Wands, merely that patience is needed as difficulties will
be overcome and all be well in the end.

FIVE OF WANDS
Conflict, competitiveness, struggle

upright

The Five of Wands is a card of unavoidable conflict and struggle. In a reading, the surrounding cards will point to the area in the querant's life where this could be a problem. This could be in almost any circumstances be it career or relationship related, as the cause will always be the same; competitiveness, frustration and a fierce determination to overcome anything or anyone in the way.

reversed

Fraud, defeat through devious means, acrimony
Serious problems and difficulties are indicated in the
querant's life, when reversed; the Five of Wands warns of
using malicious and underhand behaviour as a means of
overcoming these situations. This card also indicates
possible legal problems.

SIX OF WANDS
Victory, fulfilment, great news

upright

This card is a very welcome sight in a reading, signifying as it does, the arrival of great news, and the complete fulfilment of hopes and wishes. The hard work of the past will now bring rewards bringing, feelings of happiness and deep satisfaction. If the querant is waiting for news of the outcome of an event the Six of Wands points to an extremely positive result.

reversed

Suspicion, delayed news, anxiety
When reversed, this card signifies delayed news and
accompanying anxiety about possible outcomes.
Difficulties will arise when communicating with others
particularly work colleagues, and this could lead to
feelings of suspicion and anxiety over their motives. If
the querant is awaiting news, a reversed Six of Wands
indicates the result will not be favourable.

SEVEN OF WANDS
Challenges, courage, ultimate success

upright

The Seven of Wands upright indicates a time of great possibility for the querant. This will only become positive reality, however, if the querant faces up to challenge and potential conflict. Success will only be attained if courage and determination is exercised along with sustained effort. Stamina will also be needed as victory will not be immediate, but ultimately worthwhile. This can be linked to many areas in the querant's life such as sitting an exam, starting a new business or overcoming any serious personal struggle.

reversed

Indecisiveness, lost opportunities, timidity
When reversed the Seven of Wands points to timidity in the face of a challenge, a lack of will which ultimately will lead to defeat. Avoiding confrontation will result in a missed opportunity.

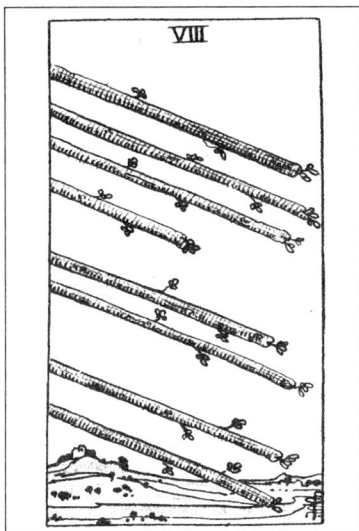

EIGHT OF WANDS
Activity, no more delays, travel

upright

This card indicates important journeys, particularly to foreign parts. It is a favourable card in a spread as it suggests the time is right for taking the initiative and grasping opportunities with confidence and courage. The pace of the querant's life will speed up as ventures begun will begin to gather momentum, and ultimately head toward a satisfactory conclusion. This card can also relate to matters of the heart, and is particularly relevant if an important decision is to be made.

reversed

Impetuous action, poor judgement, delays
Rash, impetuous action is indicated as a result of
impatience and over-eagerness to progress quicker than
is possible. This will result in wasted opportunities and
disappointment. Delays are indicated and plans may
have to be put on hold.

NINE OF WANDS
Inner strength, self-assurance

upright

This card signifies great inner strength and resourcefulness which cannot be overcome. The Nine of Wands points to courage in defence and victory in attack. Basically, the card in a reading reminds the querant to concentrate on inner strengths when facing impending difficulties. This is relevant even if the querant is in a period of relative calm in their life, the Nine of Wands indicates this will not always be the case and potential problems are on the horizon. However, by drawing on self-assurance and determination, these problems can be overcome.

reversed

Obstinacy, avoidable delays, suspicion
When reversed, the Nine of Wands points to the dangers of obstinacy and an inability to compromise. This will lead to the Querant's futile pursuit of goals and avoidable delays. A failure to move with the times and adapt to a changing world will result in squandered opportunities.

TEN OF WANDS
Pressure, over-commitment

upright

This card signifies the stresses and strains of having 'too many irons in the fire'. The querant is very likely in a position where he/she is struggling to cope with an excessive workload, with all the responsibilities this entails. There is also the added pressure of having responsibilities in the home as well as at work. It could be that the querant is unable to give both areas equal attention which has resulted in tensions. In this sense, success has become the means of oppression.

reversed

Deceit, burdens, abuse of position
When reversed, the Ten of Wands signifies the querant is unable to cope with their excessive workload. Strain, pressure, tension and anxiety are indicated. A reluctance to trust others or to hand over responsibility to another results in much of the pressure being self-inflicted and ultimately avoidable. An abuse of power is also indicated.

PAGE OF WANDS

PAGE OF WANDS
Fresh starts, loyalty, ambition

upright

The Page of Wands is a card of ambition, loyalty, enthusiasm and energy. The Page is also a messenger who brings glad tidings (in relation to a youngster), and signifies a new beginning full of hope and enthusiasm.

reversed

Vindictive character, false friendship
When reversed, the Page brings misleading information and is a spreader of gossip and malicious rumours. The card indicates superficiality, an inflated ego and disloyalty.

KNIGHT OF WANDS

KNIGHT OF WANDS
Unpredictability, intuition, travel

upright

This card describes an alert, active, unpredictable, fast moving character. Changeability is the theme of this card, the ability to seize the day and dramatically alter the course of events at a moment's notice. This character may seem to be wildly irresponsible and his behaviour startling, however, his actions are generally seen to be wise in retrospect. His energy, charm and sophisticated wit give him a magnetic personality, immensely popular with others. In readings, he can indicate an unexpected and dramatic change in the querant's circumstances, either involving foreign travel or a house move at short notice.

reversed

Conflict, premeditated arguments, travel problems
Reversed, this card symbolises the rash behaviour and the wilful destruction of order. The Knight is someone who will deliberately cause arguments and disharmony, and is known for being an egotistical, intolerant character. In a reading, the Knight is associated with prospective difficulties arising over property matters, relationships or travel.

QUEEN OF WANDS

QUEEN OF WANDS
Warm, practical, homely yet independent

upright

The woman symbolised in this card is usually mature, loving, sympathetic and fertile both physically and mentally. This can refer to the querant, or to someone who he or she can turn to or rely on in times of trouble. The Queen of Wands is generous and home-loving yet retains a strong sense of independence. She is protective of those close to her and her charm and social ease ensure her popularity .

reversed

Overbearing, matriarchal, vain
Reversed, the Queen of Wands warns of an overbearing character, who will not allow those close to her to have their independence. She is vain, and quickly imagines the worst in others. She possesses a sharp tongue and a savage wit, making her a very bad enemy indeed.

In a reading, she can also indicate possible infidelities in relationships.

KING OF WANDS

KING OF WANDS
Noble, courageous, fair, traditional

upright

The King of Wands is a mature man who is in a position of authority, be it domestic or career centred; e.g an elder relative or boss. He is admired, for he exhibits qualities of great strength and resolution. He is a lover of traditional family life and values and is a wonderful giver of moral support. He is a skilled mediator, able to see all sides in a dispute. In a reading, he can also represent a surprise windfall.

reversed

Autocratic, prejudiced, intolerant
Reversed, the King of Wands is a ruthless character, who
will stop at nothing to get what he wants. He has no
time for the opinions of others and is deeply prejudiced.
The card in a reading warns of an impending dispute
and urges the querant to be on guard.

THE SUIT OF CUPS

The Suit of Cups is associated with the emotional elements and spiritual experience in all our lives. Cups are linked with the element Water and the corresponding signs of Pisces, Taurus and Scorpio. Water is an ideal symbol for Cups as it reflects all our changing moods and emotions. Cups is associated with the suit of Hearts in an ordinary deck of cards, however it is not merely concerned with romantic issues and covers the whole range of emotions we experience such as lust, jealousy, hate, sadness and joy.

In a reading, the presence of many Cups obviously indicates the querant's emotional life is central. However, to identify a factual basis, the Reader should take the next most numerous suit into consideration, e.g. Coins could indicate financial or material concerns.

Cups are also associated with dreams and the spiritual element we all possess. As the suit is linked with the feminine 'yin' principle of nature, it indicates self-awareness, intuition and feelings of peace and fulfilment.

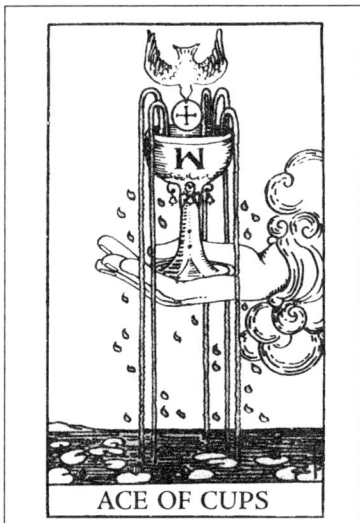

ACE OF CUPS

THE ACE OF CUPS
Contentment, creativity, faithfulness

upright

Aces signify a new beginning or chapter in the querant's life. In the case of Cups it points to an extremely positive period of fulfilment and feelings of contentment for the querant, when love, happiness and pleasure are indicated. Close, personal relationships are central as is a change in the surrounding circumstances. This can point to marriage, the birth of a child and a wonderful period of joy and plenty.

reversed

Barrenness, lost love, despair
When reversed in a spread, the Ace of Cups indicates emotional upheaval, barrenness, the stagnation of a relationship and feelings of insecurity.

TWO OF CUPS
Partnership, love, understanding

upright

The Two of Cups signifies partnership, either a strong emotional attachment current in the querant's life or one which is imminent. This strongly indicates a love affair, however, it can also be linked to business partnerships and in both cases will point to increased co-operation, harmony, and lasting happiness. In this sense it can signify the end to a feud or argument, heralding a new period of reconciliation and friendship.

reversed

Separation, divorce, betrayal
When reversed in a reading the Two of Cups indicates separation, unfaithfulness or divorce. Certainly, partnerships will be strained and then thrown away through a betrayal of trust. Jealousy and deceit are also indicated.

THREE OF CUPS
Fertility, happiness, creativity

upright

This is the card of maternity, fertility, comfort and harmony. It points to a period of great joy for the querant when good fortune will be plenty. The querant will experience wonderful feelings of happiness and a need to share his or her joy with others. Physical and emotional fulfilment are indicated, possibly the birth of a child or the happy conclusion of an important venture. The querant will feel an increase in creativity and will put this to good use.

reversed

Exploitation of others' feelings, sex without love, self-obsession
Marital problems are indicated with a reversed Three of Cups as is sex without love and the selfish exploitation of the affections of others. Positive relationships are risked due to intolerance and self-indulgence.

FOUR OF CUPS
Disillusionment, familiarity, re-evaluation

upright

The saying, 'familiarity breeds contempt' is a good way of summing up The Four of Cups as it indicates that emotional happiness and fulfilment have been attained, but instead of feeling happy and content with this state, the querant feels indifferent and bored with what he or she perceives to be the lack of excitement in life. Success has been achieved, goals have been attained, what next? This card can also indicate relationship difficulties, is love turning into habit? The querant should re-evaluate his or her life and find a new, stimulating direction.

reversed

Fatigue, ill-health through overindulgence, depression
When reversed, the four of Cups indicates the querant's dissatisfaction with their circumstances will increase, resulting in self-pity and possible depression. Overindulgence is also signified, as is fatigue and apathy. It will become increasingly difficult for the querant to work up the enthusiasm to make the necessary changes. Beware ill-health resulting from over-excess or depression.

FIVE OF CUPS
Reassessment, sense of loss, worry

upright

As depicted on this card, the cups of happiness have been overturned, leaving worry, and a sense of loss. Traditionally, fives are generally unwelcome cards in a spread, bringing with them in this instance extremely negative feelings of melancholy and disappointment. Something precious has been taken and replaced with heartache and grief. There is a positive aspect in this rather bleak interpretation which points to a need for a reappraisal of the querant's life, followed by the implementation of new strategies. The way forward is to put the regrets of the past behind and follow a new direction forward. If this can be done, there is still hope.

reversed

Worries, futility, bad luck
Bad luck is indicated with a reversed Five of Cups leaving feelings of powerlessness. Unexpected worries and problems will arise, however by putting the experiences of the past to good use, they can be overcome.

SIX OF CUPS
Harmony, happy memories, the past shaping the future

upright

This card indicates happiness and fulfilment which have been built on the efforts of the past. It could be the realisation of a dream, or a situation or person from the past which has returned and is influencing present and future enterprises/relationships. This card indicates a period of harmony, with the querant delighting in happy memories and old faces from the past including lovers.

reversed

Nostalgia, inability to face reality
Reversed, this card warns of the dangers of constantly looking back, living in the past, yearning for all that is gone and never to return. It could be the querant is hiding in the past to escape facing up to current problems which need attention.

SEVEN OF CUPS
Imagination, choice, aspirations

upright

The Seven of Cups is a card of choice. The querant could be faced with a dilemma in which there are several options to consider. To find the way forward, this card suggests responding to intuition, to appeal to the inner self. However, beware of confusion, the querant should consider his or her aims and goals carefully and establish what is realistically achievable and what is merely 'pie in the sky'.

reversed

Self-delusion, deception in matters of love

Self-delusion and a failure to face up to reality is
indicated with a reversed Seven of Cups. The querant
must avoid relying on false hopes, and instead get a grip
on reality.

EIGHT OF CUPS
Breaking of ties, development, change

upright

This card indicates a dissatisfaction with present circumstances and an urge to try something new. This could be ending an established relationship or cutting ties with the past. At the root of this is the need to progress to something new and deeper. It signifies a period of personal growth and a change of perspective. Links with the past which have ceased to be relevant will be severed.

reversed

Restlessness, dissatisfaction, unrealistic goals
Lack of considered judgement leads to the reckless
severing of long-established ties. Chasing impossible
dreams. The Eight of Cups in a reading warns against
making hasty decisions.

NINE OF CUPS
Emotional stability, kindliness, happiness

upright

This is an extremely positive card in a reading as it indicates great contentment, stability, happiness and generosity of spirit. The Nine of Cups suggests a long-cherished wish or ambition will be realised. This will leave the querant feeling extremely blessed and they will wish to share their fortune with others.

reversed

Complacency, vanity, finding faults in others
When reversed, the Nine of Cups points to complacency, vanity and conceit. In achieving ambitions, it could be the querant has succumbed to smug, self-satisfaction.

TEN OF CUPS
Commitment, peace, love

upright

An extremely positive card, the Ten of Cups signifies
dreams being realised and the great happiness and
satisfaction which follows. A secure and peaceful
environment is indicated as is the success of emotional
commitments. If the querant is considering marriage
this upright card is one of the most favourable cards to
find in a spread as it is the card of long and happy
unions, of perfect love.

reversed

Disruption of routine, antisocial behaviour
Reversed, this card indicates emotional tensions within
relationships which are normally happy. It could be the
querant is taking a partner, friend or member of the
family for granted.

PAGE OF CUPS

PAGE OF CUPS
Creativity, good advice

upright

When representative of an individual, the Page of Cups symbolises a poetic youth who is modest, reflective, gentle and artistically talented. He possesses great knowledge for one so young and will happily give advice and offer support when needed. In a spread, the Page of Cups is a positive card, and, depending on the surrounding cards can herald the arrival of good news such as a marriage or birth.

Selfish, scheming, superficial youth
When reversed, the Page points toward a superficial youth, who has much to offer on the outside with nothing deeper to support it. He has talent, but has not the stamina to pursue it, and has a lack of commitment towards others.

KNIGHT OF CUPS

KNIGHT OF CUPS
Enthusiasm, new ideas, easily bored

upright

Characteristically, the Knight of Cups represents an enthusiastic, idealistic, and amiable young man, who is often a romantic symbol in a reading. He is extremely artistic and refined, however he can be easily distracted from the task in hand, and in need of constant stimulation. In a reading, the Knight can point to new possibilities for the querant involving this character.

False friend, deviousness, fraud
A reversed Knight of Cups warns of a deceitful character and a false friend. The querant should tread carefully in both personal and business matters as problems may not be obvious at present, but will rear their head in the near future, perhaps as a result of the two-faced actions of this character.

QUEEN OF CUPS

QUEEN OF CUPS
Artistic, affectionate, intuitive

upright

The Queen of Cups represents a mature, affectionate and highly intuitive woman who is romantic in her outlook and can be trusted when her help is needed. She possesses a deep inner beauty which does not need external aids to shine. As with the other court cards in the suit of Cups, she is a relatively passive character, and can be easily influenced by events and the people she comes into contact with. She possesses an impressive artistic talent and is in touch with her inner self. In a reading she can represent a much-loved mature woman, or a reminder particularly to the male querant not to suppress their emotions.

reversed

Disloyal and unstable woman
When the Queen is reversed, she indicates a vain, fickle, deceitful woman who should be avoided. These negative aspects are not necessarily immediately obvious, and this card warns the querant to tread carefully, as she will make a troublesome enemy.

KING OF CUPS

KING OF CUPS
Mature, skilled negotiator, authoritative

upright

The King of Cups represents a mature, intelligent and well respected man. He usually holds a position of authority and is generally composed yet friendly. He is apt to hide the intensity of his true feelings underneath this rather cool exterior, and can be slightly distant or feared. He commands respect, not love, and avoids taking people into his confidence. In a reading, he generally indicates a professional adviser who will assist the querant on important matters.

reversed

Treacherous, self-centred man
As with the other court cards in this suit, the King reversed warns of a treacherous character who probably holds a position of power. His only concern is himself and his own ends, and he uses his intelligence, experience and power to exploit those around him. He would make a treacherous enemy, a major threat to be avoided at all costs.

THE SUIT OF SWORDS

Swords are the suit of intellect, and rational thought. They are concerned with justice, truth and ethical principles. Swords are associated with the astrological element Air, which symbolises light and clear thought. However, because the suit is linked with the masculine principle of yang, it indicates states of mind which can lead to disharmony, conflict, animosity and ultimate unhappiness. Swords indicate a need to seek out the truth whatever the cost, no matter who it might hurt. Hardly surprisingly, a predominance of Swords in a reading can be an alarming prospect. Traditionally, they are said to signify all things bad; death, arguments or illness, yet because they deal with the mental aspects of our character they need to be interpreted with some care. In a reading Swords reflect anxieties and concerns the querant feels toward a situation, not necessarily what is really happening. We all live in a world in which we are surrounded by stresses and strains, be they financial, emotional or career based. To interpret Swords more accurately in a reading, it is important to take into consideration the surrounding cards, and subsidiary majorities. For instance Coins will point to money worries, Wands career problems and Cups relationship difficulties. By recognising the area for concern, the querant should use Swords to point to the true way forward.

ACE OF SWORDS

ACE OF SWORDS

upright

Victory, mental clarity, necessary change

All Aces in the Minor Arcana personify the major qualities associated with their individual suits. The upright Ace of Swords is an extremely powerful card as it indicates mental clarity, and the triumph over what have appeared to be overwhelming odds. The Ace represents irresistible force, conviction and the courage to face new challenges head on. The querant may be at a point in his life where there is no going back, where there must be change to build something better. The Ace of Swords indicates the removal of all restraints and the intellectual focus and courage to make this change succeed.

reversed

Wanton destruction, misuse of power, injustice.
Reversed, the Ace indicates a complete disregard for others in the pursuit of goals. It warns of the misuse of power with dishonest and underhand dealings. Legal problems or conflicts with those in authority are also indicated. The querant may be facing a situation where the easy way out would be to abuse his position, the Ace urges, 'think again'.

TWO OF SWORDS

upright

Equilibrium, friendship in adversity, peace of mind
The Two of Swords depicts a barefoot woman wearing a blindfold, alone in the moonlight, her arms crossed, clutching two upright swords.

The image itself is unsettling, as are the majority of the Sword cards, however, ironically, the upright Two represents harmony and the balancing of two conflicting forces. From trouble and strife, comes beauty and truth. In a reading, it can signify a situation where the querant is acting as mediator in a conflict of interests, or is being forced into a position where he must choose between his heart or his head. When a resolution has been reached, it will bring an enormous sense of relief and inner peace. The Two of Swords can indicate a true friend in times of adversity, whether this is the querant holding out the hand of friendship to another or quite the reverse.

reversed

Disharmony, tension, deceit
Reversed, the Two of Swords displays all the negative aspects of the Suit. A deliberate stirring up of trouble and tension is indicated as are irreconcilable differences and the breaking down of helpful communication.

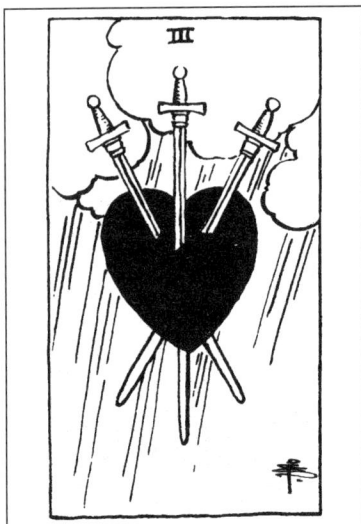

THREE OF SWORDS

This card, as illustrated, depicts a heart pierced by three swords. This disturbing image is set against a bleak sky complete with thunderous clouds and driving rain.

upright

Misery, upheaval, new beginnings
Unsurprisingly, this is generally an unhappy card. This indicates deep rooted misery and turmoil in the querant's life, most probably associated with a close personal relationship. There is much pain and conflict

surrounding the end of this partnership, and to overcome these negative feelings the querant must clear the way for what will come after. This is easier said than done, and the Three of Swords indicates that even though the future will be brighter as a result, the transition will nevertheless be a painful and alienating experience.

reversed

Discord, heartache, acrimony
Reversed, the feelings mentioned above, are enhanced, the hurt and pain felt over a separation are even more deeply felt. This will be no amicable split. The emotional trauma and potential legal wrangles will be drag on for an extended period.

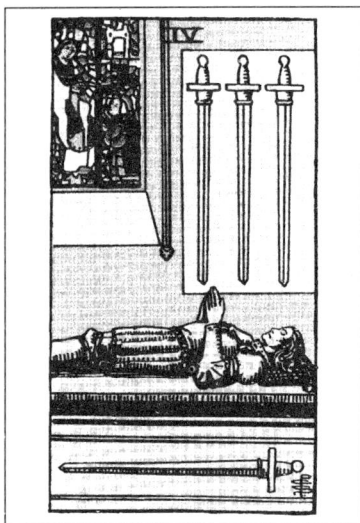

FOUR OF SWORDS

This card depicts the stained glass window of a church shining light on a stone casket with the statue of the deceased lies, hands clasped together in prayer. This is not such a disturbing image even though it indicates death, the casket is golden and a feeling of peace prevails.

upright

Healing, peace, withdrawal
The Four of Swords signifies peace, order and stability in

the midst of stress and turmoil. In a reading, it indicates that the querant will soon be enjoying respite from ongoing problems and will have time to 'recharge the batteries'. This card relates to taking care of oneself, to take the opportunity to rest and recuperate. Necessary hospitalisation is also indicated.

reversed

Exile, isolation, depression
This can indicate the querant has concentrated too much on himself and is now finding it difficult to communicate with others. This can lead to feelings of isolation and rejection. In extreme cases, this isolation is enforced indicating imprisonment.

FIVE OF SWORDS

The image on this card is one of defeat as we see three bedraggled, and desolate warriors isolated at the water's edge. The sky is full of ominous clouds, yet the figure in the foreground is picking up the swords and smiling.

upright

Wounded pride, loss, acceptance
The Five of Swords, unsurprisingly, points to defeat. The most likely interpretation is that the querant has or shortly will lose an argument or dispute with another.

To overcome the inevitable feelings of humiliation and loss, the querant must try to accept the inevitable, swallow their pride and accept defeat gracefully. Only then will it be possible to move on. Do not dwell on feelings of worthlessness and self-pity.

reversed

Treachery, spite, deceit
This card warns of impending doom as a result of underhand, malicious behaviour. If the querant is responsible for such actions, then any victory will be a hollow one. However, beware of anyone acting in such a manner when involved in your affairs, as your losses will be great.

SIX OF SWORDS

This card depicts the two huddled figures of a woman and child being rowed away over the water toward new shores.

upright

Brighter future, a journey, respite
The Six of Swords indicates better times are ahead at last. This does not mean all problems are over, but some major obstacle has been overcome and has allowed respite for the querant to progress further. This card

signifies that the path to success will not be an easy one, yet the querant can take comfort from the fact success will come eventually. The card also signifies a long journey, most probably over water to potentially more harmonious surroundings.

reversed

Failure to face up to problems, procrastination
By refusing to face up fully to problems, the querant will inevitably worsen the situation. Any attempts to run away and avoid the truth will not be successful.

SEVEN OF SWORDS

The image on the Seven of Swords is of a brightly
dressed young man tiptoeing away carrying five of the
seven swords. He is leaving something, but taking more
away, yet does not resemble the archetypal enemy.

upright

Confusion, avoidance of confrontation
The Seven of Swords advises prudence and foresight
when facing a powerful, yet unknown enemy. Someone
or something is hindering progress and the success of

plans, and the querant may not yet know their identity. The feelings associated with this are confusion and frustration and it may seem useless to continue. However, the Seven urges the querant to avoid head-on confrontation with this enemy as this will prove disastrous, but to seek out weaknesses and use practical, diligent and intelligent means instead.

reversed

Lack of nerve, indecision
Reversed, this card warns the querant not to surrender when defeat of the enemy is in sight. In short, be vigilant. Any partial victories will, at the end of the day, be meaningless, and only allow the enemy to recover ground.

EIGHT OF SWORDS

The image on the Eight of Swords is of an isolated, barefoot, and bound young woman. She is blindfolded, and stands on a beach surrounded by the eight, tall swords. Are they protecting or incarcerating her?

upright

Restriction, major difficulties, patience
The general theme of this card is frustration. The querant may be in a position where he feels is going nowhere, however, every time he tries to move his way is

blocked by circumstances outside his control. No matter how difficult this situation is to bear, it is vital to remain patient and wait for circumstances to change, otherwise disillusionment and a loss of self-belief will prevail.

reversed

Depression, hard work with little reward
With the reversed card the feelings stated above will be more acute. Frustration prevails as the querant feels trapped and isolated. Efforts will seem to make little difference.

NINE OF SWORDS

This is a card of anguish, as depicted on the card itself. The figure has woken and, sitting up in bed, covering his eyes is the epitome of misery. The black background and horizontal swords heightens the sense of desperation; problems always seem so much worse in the middle of the night, daylight can bring a clearer, brighter outlook.

upright

Disappointment, deception, shattered confidence

As indicated on the card itself, the Nine of Swords represents extreme mental pain and anguish. Confidence is at an all time low and the querant feels betrayed by those around. This may be unfounded, however it will cause great anxiety and misery. The querant may have failed at something of importance, and will experience intense feelings of disappointment and worthlessness. This card is also associated with violence and scandal, and it is imperative in a spread to carefully take into consideration the surrounding cards. The Nine can also point to illnesses and injury.

reversed

Malice, misery, isolation
Reversed, this is one of the bleakest cards in the deck. The querant is unable to escape from a desperate situation. Crippled with self-doubt, he is unable to ask for help from those who are in a position to help. This will heighten feelings of isolation and rejection.

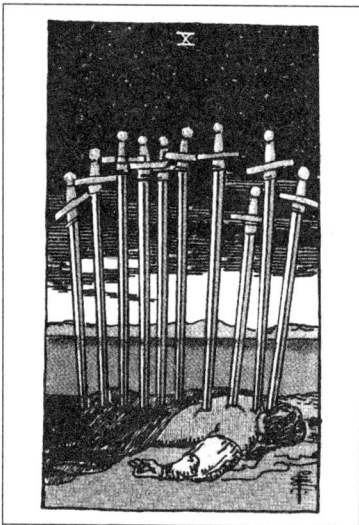

TEN OF SWORDS

The image on the Nine of Swords is at first glance deeply disturbing, depicting as it does a body lying face down on the ground having been stabbed to death. However over the water the sun is trying to break through the darkness.

upright

Desolation, ruin, anguish
This is the most dreaded card in the deck. It represents catastrophe, ruin and desolation for the querant. The

Ten of Swords symbolises the lowest point, the situation could not be worse. There is consolation in the fact that things can only get better, the worst has been experienced and, from the ashes, the querant will be able to build a new future.

reversed

False dawn, continued suffering
Reversed, this card indicates that a desperate situation for the querant is likely to get much worse. That which appears hopeful is thwarted. Traditionally the Ten of Swords represents death, however in a reading the surrounding cards should be taken into consideration when interpreting the spread, and caution should be exercised for fear of alarming the querant.

PAGE OF SWORDS

PAGE OF SWORDS

The Page, dressed in a full-sleeved tunic, stands in a relaxed pose on a hilltop, an upraised sword in his hands. The overall feeling of the card is far more optimistic than previous Sword cards. His appearance is one of elegance and social ease.

upright

Vigilance, diplomacy, intelligence
The Page signifies a vigilant youth who possesses a keen mind and wonderful analytical skills. This makes him

ideal in any debate, where he is an excellent negotiator.
He is able to recognise the truth in any situation, and is a
loyal friend and ally, particularly towards his superiors
or elders. When representing a situation, the Page
signifies change, and important decisions.

reversed

False friendship, deviousness
When reversed, the Page warns of a devious character
who will profess friendship, but will seek faults and flaws
in others often to cover up his own failings. He has no
qualms about prying into the affairs of others and is a
spiteful enemy. The querant should make every effort to
protect themselves from this character.

KNIGHT OF SWORDS

THE KNIGHT OF SWORDS

The Knight is dressed in full armour charging into battle on a fine horse. His right arm brandishes an upright sword. He looks aggressive yet focused.

upright

Courage, forcefulness, intellect
The Knight is an extremely powerful character, who possesses courage, sharp intellect and commitment. He is extremely self-assured and assertive and can at times be considered domineering. He is at his best in difficult

situations which he faces head on and therefore is a powerful ally. When describing a situation, the Knight represents a difficult period on the horizon, however if the querant is courageous and positive they will emerge victorious.

reversed

Headstrong, reckless, lack of commitment
Reversed, the Knight is a headstrong, reckless character who has no patience for details and lacks the staying power to see a difficult situation through. He is a formidable enemy who will stop at nothing for his own ends. In a situation, the card can represent negative forces outside our control such as natural disaster or illness.

QUEEN OF SWORDS

THE QUEEN OF SWORDS

The Queen of Swords is seated on an ornate throne, dressed simply yet beautifully in a robe covered in clouds against a blue sky. Her expression is stern, and on her head she wears a crown which is made of butterflies and although in her right hand she bears an upright sword, her left hand is held up in greeting.

upright

Mature woman, intelligent, independent
The Queen of Swords represents a mature woman who is

highly intelligent with a complex personality. She is concerned with fine detail and accuracy in all things. She is often a professional person such as a teacher or lawyer and her opinion is greatly valued. She is extremely self-reliant, both emotionally and financially, and is often divorced or has chosen to stay single.

reversed

Devious, dangerous enemy, critical
The Queen, when reversed, is a devious woman, who will spread malicious rumours and half-truths to further her own schemes. Her sharp tongue and fierce criticism of others make her a treacherous enemy.

KING OF SWORDS

KING OF SWORDS

In some decks, the King of Swords is dressed in full battle dress, however in the Rider-Waite deck he is a clean-shaven man simply dressed who is seated on a throne decorated with butterflies. He also holds an upright sword in his right hand and wears a simple crown.

upright

Mature man, rational, upholder of authority
The King represents a mature man who is highly

intelligent and an upholder of authority. He is usually a
professional person, whose opinion is respected, and can
represent an employer or teacher for instance. The
querant will feel they are able to approach this character
for help and assistance regarding a problem. He is an
extremely forceful character who can often be seen as
over-domineering. As a result, he finds it difficult to
form close relationships.

reversed

Calculating, bullying, impersonal
When reversed, this card warns of a cold, calculating,
deliberately cruel bully, who will exploit the querant's
weaknesses for his own ends. He is certainly capable of
deceit and will resort to aggressive tactics if this fails. In
a situation, the querant would do better to confront this
character than to run away.

THE SUIT OF PENTACLES

Pentacles, (also known as Coins) identify with practicality, security and material wealth, but can also represent the querant's feelings of self-worth and values of a non-materialistic nature. The suit corresponds to the feminine element of Earth and celebrates the beauty of nature, and the physical experiences associated with it. Coins can initially seem the most straightforward of all the suits to interpret, however, although they indicate financial or material gains and losses, it should not be assumed that this will bring corresponding happiness or sadness to the querant's life. The surrounding cards and subsidiary suits will have great bearing on the reading.

ACE OF PENTACLES

ACE OF PENTACLES

This image on the card is of a hand appearing from the sky cupping the single pentacle. The scene beneath is of a garden in bloom and the overall feeling of the card is one of optimism.

upright

Security, wealth, recognition
All Aces symbolise new beginnings and in this case the Ace of Coins points to an extremely fruitful period for the querant which will result in financial gain and

immense satisfaction. This can also take the form of a promotion, where the querant will be recognised for their efforts. This will bring a sense of worth both materially and emotionally. The card indicates an appreciation of the good things in life; stable relationships and emotional security. A deep sense of contentment is signified.

reversed

Greed, superficiality, self-obsession
Reversed, this card warns the querant of the dangers of becoming obsessed with material comforts and the acquisition of wealth. The Ace represents greed, miserliness and complete dependence on physical pleasures in order to be happy. The querant is not in touch with his inner self and has become self-absorbed in the pursuit of power and influence.

TWO OF PENTACLES

This card depicts a young man, probably a jester or fool, performing some sort of juggling with the two coins. He seems to be concentrating on the job in hand and behind him sail two galleons on the high seas.

upright

Changing fortunes, journeys, foresight
Upright, the Two of Coins is a card of change. This represents the natural fluctuations in fortune which

must be planned for. This card signifies a need for balance between the positive and negative aspects of a prospective change in circumstances. Financial gain is indicated, but careful management of funds is advised. On the whole this is a positive card, which indicates much activity connected with business opportunities, such as journeys, news and material matters. Good fortune is on its way, however it will not all be 'plain sailing', skilful navigation is needed.

reversed

Distractions, impending trouble, inconsistency
When reversed, this card warns against disregarding good advice, a lack of focus and disorganisation when dealing with fluctuating fortunes. Long term success is put to one side in favour of pleasures of the moment, and inconsistent actions negate any progress. Overindulgence in physical pleasures is also signified.

THREE OF PENTACLES

This card depicts a craftsman at work in a church, in consultation with a monk and what appears to be an architect holding plans. The overall feeling of this card is teamwork.

upright

Recognition, teamwork, prosperity
The upright Three of Coins is the card of the worker, craftsman or businessman. Although it signifies recognition and success in business ventures for the

querant it also represents being part of a team and the important part each number plays in working together in order to succeed. This card signifies building future prosperity and rightly rewards skill and effort. Any project which commences at this time will succeed.

reversed

Delays, criticism, bitterness
The card when reversed, indicates hard work yet results in disappointment and failure. This could be the result of poor planning at the beginning, when good advice was ignored and firm foundations were not laid. The querant feels bitterness towards those who offer advice or criticism, even those they respects.

FOUR OF PENTACLES

On the card a nobleman sits on a simple plinth clutching a coin. There are coins placed above his head and beneath both his feet. Behind him is a thriving town.

upright

Emotional and material security, contentment
This is an extremely welcome card in a reading as it signifies complete material stability. The Four of Coins indicates financial gain will come either from a successful business venture or from an inheritance or

gift. Status is heightened and the querant will experience contentment as both emotional and material needs are being satisfied.

reversed

Greed, indecision, material obsession
When reversed, the Four indicates problems caused by material obsession, resulting in greed and miserliness. Opposition to change is also signified as the querant is terrified of losing what has been gained.

FIVE OF PENTACLES

This is a desolate card. The figures are in rags, one a cripple, the other a woman huddled against the driving blizzard. Above, the window shines brightly with the five coins, yet the two characters' heads are turned away.

upright

Unemployment, financial worries, relationship difficulties
Unsurprisingly, this is not a promising card to draw as it indicates struggle and hardship. This could be as a result

of unemployment or the failing of a business venture.
This will place strains on personal relationships and
emotionally this will be a very stressful time for the
querant. This all looks incredibly bleak, but there is light
at the end of the tunnel, and by forming a bond with
others in the same situation, a way forward will become
apparent.

reversed

Hard times, potential health concerns
When reversed, the card indicates all the problems listed
above will be even harsher or take longer to resolve. The
querant will suffer under such pressure and as a result
may become ill. A new direction is imperative; to stay
on the old path will only bring ruin. It is time to fully
face up to facts: only then can the rebuilding start.

SIX OF PENTACLES

This card depicts a wealthy nobleman, scales in his left hand, dispensing money to two beggars crouched at his feet. His expression is gentle.

upright

Charity, prosperity, balance
This card indicates balance and solvency in material affairs. The querant will achieve great success and financial rewards are imminent. With the gratitude of one who knows they have been blessed with good

fortune, the querant will use their wealth to help others.
Generosity and a kind heart are indicated.

reversed

Loss, careless money management
All the positive indications of the upright Six are
reversed. Reckless money management will result in
self-induced financial problems. Although financial loss
is indicated the Six can also refer to a close personal
relationship which will be put under severe strain.

SEVEN OF PENTACLES

A field worker stands leaning on his hoe, looking disdainfully at the huge crop he has to attend to.

upright

Perseverance, sustained effort, eventual success
This card indicates eventual success but only through sustained effort. At the moment, the rewards may seem very far off and it will be difficult to keep up momentum, however if the querant perseveres their efforts will eventually be rewarded.

reversed

Failed opportunities, despondency, self-induced money problems
The querant will become despondent, frustrated and will give in to the problems surrounding them. They will lose faith in the future, abandoning their goals and therefore put themselves in financial jeopardy.

EIGHT OF PENTACLES

A craftsman works away carving the coins which are stacked up the side of a tree. The man is absorbed in his work.

upright

Change in fortune, craft skills, satisfaction
There will be a change for the better in financial matters. The querant will either put a skill to good use or discover a new area for development. These skills will bring a sense of value and pleasure not necessarily

associated with material wealth, but labour will bring rewards.

The Eight urges the querant to exercise caution where money matters are concerned, as they will be grateful for this in the future. This is an extremely promising card for anyone with artistic talent and enthusiasm.

reversed

Lack of direction, squandered opportunities
This card when reversed warns against concentrating on immediate returns at the expense of long-term success. Squandered opportunities are indicated as is dishonesty in business affairs.

NINE OF PENTACLES

This is a bright, optimistic image. A solitary young
woman dressed in robes stands in relaxed pose in a
beautiful garden. A bird of paradise has landed on her
gloved, left hand.

upright

Material success, achievement, solitude
Great success has been achieved and satisfaction is
sweeter as this has been the result of much effort. The
querant now enters a period of fulfilment, and

considerable material gains. As indicated on the card itself, solitude is signified. It could be that the querant chooses to celebrate their success alone or that they are yet to form a close personal partnership.

reversed

Devious means, financial instability
When reversed, the Nine reminds the querant not to take current financial security for granted. This could refer to wealth attained by devious means, or through the exploitation of others.

TEN OF PENTACLES

This is a welcome card in a spread. A young couple stand under an archway surrounded by the Ten Coins. There are indications throughout indicating security, family and contentment. A young child stands close to the woman, there are two dogs, and an old man sits in the foreground.

upright

Inheritance, family ties, emotional security
Upright, the Ten of Coins indicates emotional and

material security brought about by a close family bond. It could be the querant will inherit, or be given a financial gift, from a relative. The term 'blood is thicker than water' is especially apt in this case. The carrying on of family traditions is indicated.

reversed

Financial problems, family restrictions
When reversed, the Ten warns of the possible restrictions placed on the querant by family obligations and expectations. There may be a legal dispute surrounding the breaking-up of an estate after a death.

PAGE OF PENTACLES

PAGE OF PENTACLES

A young man in a broad-brimmed hat stands confidently on open land holding a large coin.

upright

Sound business sense, honourable, conscientious
When upright, this card indicates a young man who has all the above qualities and who is proud of the responsibilities he carries. He is particularly linked with a creative, artistic life and generally signals good news for the querant. He enjoys challenge, and will apply

himself to the task in hand to the best of his potential.
Excellent exam results or promotions are indicated.

reversed

*Potential money problems, lack of humour, lack of
application*
When reversed, the Page indicates an idle young man
who lacks the application needed to progress for himself,
or in the service of others. He is wasteful of
opportunities which come his way and indicates bad
news where money matters are concerned.

KNIGHT OF PENTACLES

KNIGHT OF PENTACLES

The Knight sits motionless in full battle dress and holding a large coin surveying the wide open land around.

upright

Defender of truth, honourable, practical
The Knight is the defender of what we believe to be right and true. He is an honourable, dependable young man who will be a staunch ally in times of trouble or in a work environment. He upholds tradition and has a

cautious and responsible outlook on life. The Knight also indicates that good news regarding finances will be brought by a young man, or come about because of him.

reversed

Smug, complacent, unmotivated young man
When reversed, the Knight warns of the dangers of being overcautious. This is when careful action develops into complacency, and a lack of foresight. He dislikes progress and will slow the querant down with his lack of motivation.

QUEEN OF PENTACLES

QUEEN OF PENTACLES

The Queen sits on her throne in a lush garden, holding a
large coin. Above her head is an arch of roses.

upright

Financially responsible, shrewd, down-to-earth
The Queen is a practical, down-to-earth woman who
has many wonderful qualities. She is wise and
compassionate, yet loves the good things in life such as
comfort and splendour. She is a warm and forgiving
character, who has marvellous financial insight, and her

advice on money matters is to be depended on.

reversed

Materialistic, suspicious, insecure
When reversed, the Queen indicates an overly
materialistic mature woman whose whole life is
governed by her possessions. She may use this
outpouring of wealth to mask the fact that she is deeply
insecure. She has a narrow outlook and is suspicious of
anything she does not understand. In financial matters,
the querant would do well to avoid this character as she
will cause nothing but trouble.

KING OF PENTACLES

KING OF PENTACLES

The King of Coins is also seated on a fine throne
outside. His castle is visible in the background and he
holds a large coin in one hand, his sceptre in the other.
His cloak is covered with vines and grapes and he is
surrounded by flowers and nature.

upright

Down-to-earth, reliable, trustworthy, patient
The King is a practical, down-to-earth mature man who
is by nature dependable and loyal. He may not be

particularly intelligent, but is capable of shrewd and effective judgement especially in financial matters. In a reading, the King can signify an improvement in the querant's finances or a promotion at work.

reversed

Materialistic, insensitive, jealous
When the King is reversed, it warns the querant of a dull, materialistic and foolish man. He may well be a work associate who harbours jealous feelings towards the querant, and who could cause problems. He is insensitive and shallow, only interested in people who can give him something.

GLOSSARY

Cartomancy
the practice of fortune telling through reading cards

Coins
a suit of the Minor Arcana, also known as Pentacles.
Associated with the element Earth, and issues concerning
material aspects.

Court Cards
the Kings, Queens, Knights and Pages of the Minor Arcana

Cup
a suit of the Minor Arcana. Associated with the element
Water and issues concerning emotions and affairs of the
heart.

Deck
the pack of cards

Divination
the process of predicting the future

Divinatory meaning
the interpretation of the cards and their implications for the

querant

Major Arcana
the dominant first twenty-two cards in the Tarot deck.

Minor Arcana
the remaining 56 cards divided into four suits of 14

Occult
the supernatural

Pentacles
one of the suits of the Minor Arcana also known as Coins, linked with the element Earth, and concerned with material wealth.

Querant
the person who the reading is for

Reading
the interpretation of the Tarot layout

Significator
the card chosen to represent the querant in a reading

Spread
the layout of the cards for divination purposes

Suit
one of the four sets of the Minor Arcana

Swords

a suit of the Minor Arcana. Linked with the element Air, it is concerned with intellectual activity.

Wands

a suit of the Minor Arcana. Linked with the element Fire, it is concerned with career matters.

USEFUL ADDRESSES

Mysteries
9-11 Monmouth Street
Covent Garden
London
WC2 9DA

Tel: 020 7240 3688
Fax: 020 7240 4845
E-mail: info@mysteries.co.uk

Somerville of Edinburgh
82 Canongate
The Royal Mile
Edinburgh
EH8 8BZ

Tel: 0131 556 5225
Fax: 0131 557 9305
E-mail: cards@playing-cards.demon.co.uk
Web-site: www.playing-cards.demon.co.uk

US Games Systems Inc
179 Ludlow Street
Stamford
Ct 06902
USA

Tel: 00 1 203 353 8400
E-mail: usgames@aol.com

Occultique
73 Kettering Road
Northampton
NN1 4AW

Tel: 01604 627727
(Mail order only)

Waterstones Bookstore
116 New Street
Birmingham
B2 4JJ

Tel: 0121 631 4333
Fax: 0121 643 2441
E-mail: birmingham-newstreet.waterstones.co.uk

Pentagram
11 Cheapside
Wakefield
WF1 2SD

Tel: 01294 298930
Fax: 01294 298930
E-mail: pentagrame@psinet.demon.co.uk
Web site: w www.psinet.co.uk